COLORADO
OUTLAWS & LAWMEN

COLORADO OUTLAWS & LAWMEN

— FRONTIER FOES AND HEROES —

Nancy K. Williams

Published by The History Press,
An imprint of Arcadia Publishing
Charleston, SC
www.historypress.com

Copyright © 2025 by Nancy K. Williams
All rights reserved

First published 2025

Manufactured in the United States

ISBN 9781467157957

Library of Congress Control Number: 2025931726

Notice: The information in this book is true and complete to the best of our knowledge. It is offered without guarantee on the part of the author or The History Press. The author and The History Press disclaim all liability in connection with the use of this book.

All rights reserved. No part of this book may be reproduced or transmitted in any form whatsoever without prior written permission from the publisher except in the case of brief quotations embodied in critical articles and reviews.

To Tom—for always helping.
To Wendy—for understanding.
I miss the good times.
In memory of Danny and Chip-Chip

CONTENTS

ACKNOWLEDGEMENTS

hanks to Tom Williams for his original photographs of Colorado and Utah and for compiling and editing the historic photographs used in this book.

Following the trails of these determined lawmen and wily outlaws has been an interesting journey. There are conflicting stories and opinions about several individuals in this book. Some newspapers told true stories, and others slanted them and blatantly distorted facts. Local historical societies and museums with old newspaper clippings, original manuscripts and notes have been very helpful in separating fact from fiction.

The Museum of the West, the Museum of Northwest Colorado, and the Delta County Historical Society Museum have important collections of historic photographs, documents, and memorabilia that are pertinent to the events described in this book. My thanks to History Colorado, the Wyoming Historical Society, and other regional historical societies and libraries for their assistance and information.

INTRODUCTION

When violence erupted in the West, it often occurred in the mining camps or during range wars among the large cattle ranchers and homesteaders. In 1859, the Pikes Peak Gold Rush brought thousands to Colorado who hoped to find their fortunes. As they scrambled up steep canyons and waded through icy streams, the lucky ones found gold and staked their claims. Thieves were right behind them to steal or jump those claims. Life in a mining camp was rough; men, liquor, disappointment, and guns came together here to create violence.

Miners did not want rule by knife or gun, and there was a need for a system of law and order to protect everyone's rights. Mining districts were organized, and rules were established to govern the way they would operate and live together. Thieves and predators who didn't follow the rules found themselves in miners' courts, where they were tried and judged by their peers—and justice was served. Occasionally, an innocent man was hanged.

If a newcomer wasn't a Fifty-Niner looking for gold, he wanted land. At first, there was plenty, and it was free. Charles Goodnight brought the first Texas longhorns over the Goodnight-Loving Trail to Colorado in 1866. The cattle business grew in the 1870s as stockmen built their herds. Homesteaders came and fenced their land, decreasing the range for cattle. Large ranchers began pushing the smaller ranchers, homesteaders, and sheepmen out and seizing their land.

Cattle and horses, the most tangible form of wealth, were the targets of thieves. The most common crime on the Colorado plains was cattle rustling, and brands were changed easily. The arrival of the railroads made it easier to get stolen cattle to market. Homesteaders were often accused of rustling, and lynching was sometimes the ranchers' solution.

When sheep came to the Western Slope, their grazing habits ruined the land. The range wars over sheep were vicious in Colorado and Wyoming and lasted through the early days of the twentieth century. Men were killed, and thousands of sheep were slaughtered.

Farmers and businessmen, who settled along the Front Range, wanted stability that fostered economic growth. The railroads brought the raw materials necessary for development and supported growth, but they also brought thieves and con men, gamblers, and ladies of the evening.

Stagecoach robbers were a cut above pickpockets and stickup artists, who robbed people on the street and travelers on lonely roads. Stagecoaches carrying gold and silver shipments were some of the first outlaw targets. While traveling through lonely, unsettled regions, their only security was their driver and a shotgun-wielding guard.

After the railroad arrived, the express car became a rolling bank, its safes loaded with cash and shipments of gold and valuable metals. Slow-moving trains were easily stopped, and if needed, dynamite could blast open their express cars.

It became obvious that regions in Colorado must be organized with rules and laws, and someone was needed to enforce them. At first, the man sworn in as the sheriff was equipped with a horse, a gun, and a tin badge. He needed courage, the ability to shoot straight, and some reasoning and detective skills to handle the job competently. He had no training to help him succeed. As the years passed and men like Dave Cook and Doc Shores became lawmen, a legal system was established in which the law prevailed, even in those wild times.

1

DAVE COOK

HANDS UP! THE ROCKY MOUNTAIN DETECTIVE AGENCY

Dave Cook was nineteen years old in 1859, when he witnessed the lynching of a prospector who stole a bag of gold dust. Justice was swift in the Colorado mining camps, and the prisoner was provided a lawyer, and a judge was selected from the camp residents. The thief was found guilty and sentenced to hang, and the sentence was carried out swiftly. Dave was troubled that justice was delivered so quickly that an innocent man could be hanged. He never dreamed he would eventually play a part in revolutionizing the law enforcement system in the Rocky Mountains.

Cook and his younger brother worked their mining claim near Black Hawk and accumulated a small bag of gold, enough to tide them through the winter of 1859–60. Disaster struck when a thief stole it, but Dave was determined to get their gold back. He methodically followed the clues and caught the thief in Golden. Knowing he might be hanged for this crime, the thief begged for his life, and Dave decided to let him go after he retrieved his gold.

When the Civil War broke out in 1861, the Cook brothers sold their mining claim and went home to Kansas. Dave went to work for the Union army and was put in charge of military supply trains in Missouri. He found out that ammunition, guns, and supplies were being stolen before they could reach the troops. Dave tracked the thieves down, arrested them, and turned them over to the army.

Recognizing Cook's detective ability, the army transferred him to the quartermaster corps in the Army of the Frontier, where there was a staggering number of thefts. It took a month for Dave to expose the large ring of civilians and enlisted men who were stealing and selling army supplies. After he caught thieves who were stealing guns and ammunition from the ordnance department, he was transferred to Denver as assistant to the U.S. government's chief detective, Alden Warwick. His first assignment was to stop the theft of horses and supplies from the Colorado Military District.

David J. Cook, western American lawman and city marshal of Denver, Colorado, responsible for over three thousand arrests. *Public domain.*

Cook worked undercover and rented a room in a cheap boardinghouse in the rough part of Denver. He made the rounds of saloons and shady hangouts, making friends with gang members and local toughs. He became friendly with two thugs known as "Google-Eye" and "Smiley" and learned they were buying supplies and stolen army horses from soldiers. After horse thefts, Smiley and Google-Eye sold the animals to a saloon keeper and disappeared. The detectives were determined to find out what happened to those horses.

Cook instructed a trusted soldier to steal an army horse and then sell it to the saloonkeeper. After the soldier had been paid and left, an accomplice jumped on the stolen horse and galloped out of town. Cook and Frank Smith followed him and spent more than fifteen hours riding across one hundred miles of rough country. The accomplice finally stopped in a remote valley, where he met two men. Cook and Smith moved quickly taking the thieves by surprise, ordering, "Hands up!" Fifteen army horses were grazing nearby, and the trio outdid themselves spilling information about their operation in hopes of escaping the hangman's rope. The detectives learned that this gang was also involved in a burglary and holdup ring in Denver. The thieves received inside information from employees, laborers, and handymen about wealthy targets who had valuables hidden in their homes. Servants tipped them off when homeowners were gone for the evening or were out of town. Then the robbers went into action and quickly made off with the goods. Google-Eye and Smiley stored the stolen property in a Denver warehouse until it could be sold.

Cook and Smith returned to Denver and developed a plan with Warwick to round up these criminals. Three squads of cavalrymen raided the warehouse and the robbers' favorite hangouts, arresting the thieves, saloonkeepers, and the ringleaders, Google and Smiley. The army recovered many stolen horses and some of the stolen property. The criminals were sentenced to territorial prison, but Smiley and Google-Eye escaped after serving a little time. They were tracked down by a vigilante posse and lynched.

When Warwick retired, Cook took over as the chief government detective for the Quartermaster's Department for Northern Colorado and served until the Civil War ended. In 1866, he was elected Denver city marshal by a landslide, and he appointed W. Frank Smith as his chief deputy.

Historian William Collier described Cook's mind as a "veritable photographic file," commenting that the lawman never forgot a face. He studied portraits, images, and descriptions of criminals to record their features in his memory. Outlaws often surrendered to Cook rather than fight because they knew he wouldn't hesitate to shoot if necessary. He believed justice should be tempered with mercy but never leniency.

In the 1860s, lawmen were responsible for solving all the crimes that occurred in their county or municipality. They tracked down and arrested the guilty, no matter how far they fled. Jurisdictions and boundaries were often unclear, and lawmen weren't always willing to work together. The telephone wasn't invented until 1877, and it took years to get service in many areas. Some lawmen operated on both sides of the law, and crimes often went unsolved as perpetuators escaped punishment. Angry citizens formed vigilance committees and took matters into their own hands, delivering justice at the end of a rope. Unfortunately, these vigilantes sometimes hanged an innocent man.

The crime called "The Italian Murders" increased tensions in Denver and added to the hostility against Italian immigrants. They were viewed as drunken mobsters, and everyone believed crime would increase if Italians continued to come to the city. In October 1875, everyone began complaining about the terrible stench on Larimer Street. On October 20, Officer Sherman and the residents of the neighborhood started a search to find the cause. The odor and thick swarms of flies drew them to a vacant building where they saw pools of blood on the floor. Bloody handprints and splatters of blood on the walls led them to a trapdoor in the kitchen floor, where narrow stairs went down to a dark cellar. The foul smell was overpowering here. Using a candle for light, they discovered a pile of filthy blankets and a blood-soaked mattress in a dark corner. Under the mattress, there were four decaying corpses, five bloody knives, a hatchet smeared with blood and hair, and a razor. Three violins, two harps, and a scissor-sharpening machine had been tossed on top of the gruesome heap.

The victims had been stabbed multiple times, and their throats had been cut. Despite their advanced decomposition, the neighbors were able to identify the bodies by their clothing. A shoemaker, Giuseppe "Uncle Joe" Pecorra, was identified by his shoes. The other victims were his two sons and a cousin who were Italian musicians, and they'd all been living in the building. Their bodies were hauled away in a wagon and quickly buried in potters' field. A crowd of angry citizens burned the house down, and there were rumors that the killers were Italians. This aggravated the tense ethnic relations already present in Denver. The story of the murders appeared in newspapers nationwide, and the killers were described as "butchers," "snarling mongrels," and "Italian gorillas."

Dave Cook, now the sheriff of Arapaho County, theorized that robbery was the motive for the killings. He asked questions around the neighborhood and learned the victims had often been seen with Filomeno Gallotti and Michele Bellotti, who were members of a gang called the "Italian Banditti," or the "Italian Butchers." Moving quickly, Cook found out these two men had been seen boarding a southbound train the day after the murders. He theorized that they were probably headed for Mexico. Cook sent detectives Frank Smith and R.Y. Force after them. They arrived in Trinidad, Colorado, on October 26 and tracked Michele Ballotti, Silvestro Campagne, and Leonard Alessandri to a saloon owned by an Italian. The officers took the three suspects to the Trinidad Jail for questioning and discovered that two of them were wearing bloodstained undershirts. They learned that Bellotti left his soiled undershirt at the saloon. The trio had fifty dollars in cash and twenty dollars in gold coins. When they were questioned, Alessandri confessed that six men had killed Uncle Joe and the boys, but he insisted he had no part in the crimes.

Cook expanded his search for the other suspects into New Mexico, while his officers worked out a way to trick the fugitives. Smith disguised himself as a wealthy sheep owner and wore an expensive suit, while dark-complexioned Force pretended to be a laborer looking for his Italian partners. The officers tracked Filomeno Gallotti and John Arratti to Taos, where they'd purchased a gun with gold coins. They were arrested, and a third suspect, Henry Fernandez, was captured. They were taken back to Denver, and three more fugitives: Frank Valendre, Leonard Deodato, and a man known as the Ranchman were arrested.

The nine Italian Banditti were tried for the murders of the four musicians in May 1876, and they pleaded guilty to avoid execution. Gallotti, Ballotti, and Valendre were sentenced to life in prison, while the others were given

The original badge of the Rocky Mountain Detective Association. *Rocky Mountain Detective Association, Everett D. Graff Collection of Western Americana (Newberry Library).*

lighter sentences. The public was outraged that they escaped execution because of a legal technicality.

Dave Cook believed crime fighting in Colorado could be improved. He recruited seventy-five men known for their reliability and integrity, who became the first members of the Rocky Mountain Detective Association. They agreed to share information and evidence and to work together to arrest criminals. Unlike a vigilance committee, they would commit no lynching. Cook hoped the organization would recruit more members nationwide and become an efficient crime fighting tool.

The Rocky Mountain Detective Association expanded, and by 1867, the Wyoming Territory and Utah were participating. Kansas followed, and connections with Nebraska, New Mexico, Arizona, California, and the Pacific Northwest developed. In the east, well-known detectives and police officials became "agents" of the Rocky Mountain Detective Association, which expanded into the most effective crime-fighting organization in the country.

In Colorado, rustling ranked with theft and murder as one of the most serious crimes. Cattle were disappearing so rapidly that the Stock Growers Association, headquartered in Denver, hired Cook to investigate and catch the rustlers. Cook did his research and sent his report to the association with the suggestion that it be read aloud at their meeting. This document named the principal officers and several members of the association as some of the boldest cattle thieves. The culprits rushed out of the meeting amid the angry shouts of the members who demanded that they return their stolen cattle. Dave Cook was paid, and disgusted members disbanded the organization.

To speed up the recovery of rustled cattle or stolen horses, Cook announced that if he was notified within twenty-four hours of a theft, he'd recover the animals or pay for them himself. This pledge was challenged and led to one of the most grueling tasks Cook faced in his law enforcement career. On a frigid December morning in 1867, two valuable horses were stolen in Denver, and the thieves, George Britt and William Hilligoss, headed toward Boulder. Dave and another marshal followed, but the thieves gave them the slip. The marshals returned to Denver, and Cook learned the pair had headed east. So, he quickly grabbed a seat on the first stagecoach going toward Kansas.

Wearing a bulky stage drivers' coat and slouch hat, Cook rode on the box with the driver so the thieves wouldn't recognize him. He learned that two men who fit their descriptions had rested their horses at a station along the road. The stage continued east for two hundred miles, and the rough road, cramped seats, and frigid temperature made it impossible to sleep. As they neared Fort Wallace, Kansas, Cook spied the two horse thieves riding just ahead. He told the driver to speed up, pass them, go a little farther and then stop. Then Cook and the driver jumped off the box and acted like something was wrong with the stage. When the two horsemen rode up, Cook whirled around, gun raised, and ordered, "Hands up!" The surprised thieves dropped their guns and dismounted, and they were quickly handcuffed. The lawman commanded, "March!" He made his angry prisoners walk to Fort Wallace, where he spent another sleepless night guarding them.

When morning came, Cook loaded his prisoners into the first Denver-bound freight wagon. They sat on the bare boards of the wagon floor since there were no seats. Cook was exhausted, having been on their trail for four sleepless nights, so his prisoners watched him closely, hoping he'd fall asleep. They bounced about all day in the subzero weather, and when it grew dark, Cook did doze off. He roused quickly when he felt his gun being stealthily eased out of its holster. He grabbed the weapon, which George Britt was trying to nab with his feet. Cook yelled for the driver to stop and asked him for a candle. When the surly man refused to hand one over, Cook told him he could either give him a candle or carry two dead bodies to Denver. The prisoners suddenly realized that the exasperated marshal really would shoot them and pleaded for a candle. The disagreeable driver finally gave Cook one which he lit and secured safely. He grimly warned the outlaws, "One move, and I'll shoot you." The pair knew he meant it and sat quietly until they reached Denver, where Cook, exhausted and chilled to the core, locked them in a jail cell. He had been gone five days with little sleep, but the stolen horses had been recovered. He went to bed and slept seventeen hours. Britt and Hilligoss were tried and sentenced to three years in prison, but they escaped after serving one year and were never heard of again.

Cook's determined detective work kept crime under control in Denver, but crime rates had increased in the neighboring cow towns and railroad shipping centers. As part of the Rocky Mountain Detective Association, he wanted to develop ways in which lawmen in different regions could share information about criminal activity and work together to catch the perpetrators. The development of such a system was vital in early 1868, when forty horses were stolen from a Colorado breeder. This was followed by the theft of a large number of horses in Texas, Kansas, and Arizona. Law enforcement officials in these different regions didn't know that similar crimes had been committed in other states at the same time. Dave Cook realized that this was organized crime on a large scale. The horse thefts and robberies followed a pattern, and Cook concluded that one person was responsible for organizing this entire group of gangs and outlaws. He shared this information with other lawmen and was determined to shut down this large criminal ring. Cook advised all lawmen to watch horse and stock sales in their region, track the sellers, and gather information about all local horse thefts. Putting all this data together, he concluded that the huge crime ring was headquartered in Denver. He found out the leader was Lewis Musgrove, who'd been a wanted man for two years. Musgrove was working with Jack Willetson and Ed Franklin, both killers who were wanted in multiple states.

Cook investigated Musgrove's background and learned he'd gone to California in the 1849 gold rush. While in Napa, he killed a man in an argument about the Civil War and fled to Nevada. After killing two men there, he headed for Wyoming, where he shot another man at Fort Halleck. He was arrested and tried in Denver for this crime but was released on a technicality. By 1864, Musgrove was leading a gang of outlaws, stealing horses and cattle from the military. Then they expanded to rustling horses on the open range. They drove the animals two hundred to five hundred miles on established routes through isolated regions where there were few homesteads or towns. The horses were delivered to a railroad depot, shipped to profitable markets and sold. Texas horses were often sold in Colorado, while horses stolen in Utah might be sold in Wyoming. Once the stolen horses were sold, the outlaws immediately stole more animals from that same area. Sometimes, horses that had just been sold were stolen again, then driven back to their home region, where they were sold once more.

A robbery ring was associated with the horse thieves, and occasionally, after the stolen horses had been sold, the robbery ring would break into the homes of wealthy citizens and steal cash and valuables. Since Musgrove was constantly moving around, supervising activities, he set up a communication center in a Denver saloon. He often left messages there for Franklin and Willetson to coordinate their raids.

After Cook and other lawmen began intercepting the ring's messages and learned about upcoming operations, some of Musgrove's outlaw gangs were captured, while others were broken up and scattered. Ten of Musgrove's closest allies were arrested, and two outlaws who stole horses were lynched in Cheyenne. By the end of July 1868, Musgrove's syndicate could no longer manage the sale of stolen horses or coordinate the activities of the robbery ring. Musgrove abandoned his headquarters and message center in Denver and fled, while members of the detective association stayed alert and watched for him.

On October 28, 1868, Lewis Musgrove was captured after he and sixteen men disguised as Indians robbed the Union Pacific at Elk Mountain in southern Wyoming. They killed four men and even scalped two before they rode off, stealing sixteen mules. Musgrove escaped but was quickly recaptured. He was placed in manacles and leg irons and escorted to Denver by forty soldiers and jailed to await trial. He managed to get word to his gang that he needed help.

During this time, Ed Franklin, Musgrove's right-hand man, was tracked down by troopers after he stole some mules from a Wyoming army post. There was a prolonged gun fight in which the outlaw held them off for seventeen hours but was shot and finally surrendered. Franklin was taken to the army fort, where his wound was treated, and he recovered enough to eventually escape and head for Denver to help Musgrove.

Along the way, Franklin met Sanford Duggan, a petty criminal, and they traveled together to Denver. Franklin gathered about twenty outlaws together and made a plan to break Musgrove out of jail. Since they needed money, Franklin and Duggan robbed several Denver citizens, and one of their victims was Judge Brooks. He handed over his money, $135. One of his bills was torn and had been repaired with a piece of the judge's official stationery. Cook told the association members about this patched bill so everyone could watch for it.

In just two days, the bill was passed in a Golden saloon, so Cook quickly organized a posse and rode there. Franklin was sleeping off a drunken binge at the Overland Hotel while Duggan was still drinking in Hill's saloon. Cook, Smith, and their men headed that way, but they were spotted, and Duggan began shooting at them. He escaped into the night, but Miles Hill, the popular brother of the saloon keeper, was killed. The posse and a group of townspeople searched the steep, brushy hillsides around Golden, but Duggan had disappeared.

Dave Cook, Frank Smith, and Golden's Sheriff Keith went to the hotel where Franklin was staying and were directed to the outlaw's room. Franklin woke as they entered and grabbed the gun he had tucked under his pillow.

The killing of Ed Franklin at Golden by Officers Cook and Smith. He was killed while resisting arrest. *A.P. Proctor illustration from* Hands Up, *by David J. Cook.*

There was a violent struggle, and Cook and Frank Smith both fired, killing the outlaw.

Musgrove had been boasting for days: "My boys are getting me out of here!" This infuriated hundreds of Denver citizens, who gathered at the jail. This was not a loud, unruly mob; instead, it was a quiet group of doctors, lawyers, businessmen, and prominent citizens who were determined to put an end to this major criminal threat. They entered the jail, met no resistance, and dragged Musgrove out of his cell. The large crowd marched him to the Larimer Street bridge over Cherry Creek. Musgrove realized this was the end and asked for time to write notes to his wife and friends. Then he smoked one last cigarette and was hanged. When the members of his gang heard their boss had been lynched, they wasted no time getting out of Denver.

Cook notified association members about Duggan, and he was captured near Cheyenne. Cook brought him back to Denver, where another lynch mob was waiting to grab this prisoner. Cook held them off with a six-shooter in each hand and got Duggan safely locked in a cell. The mob slowly dispersed, and Cook told his staff that the outlaw would be moved after dark

Lynching of Musgrove.

The lynching of Musgrove at Cherry Creek Bridge, Denver. *A.P. Proctor illustration from* Hands Up, *by David J. Cook.*

to the more secure Denver City Jail. He said this was a confidential plan, and no one else was to know.

Late that night, Cook sent a wagon to smuggle Duggan to the Denver City Jail. The prisoner was hidden in a wagon, but while en route to the large jail, a swarm of armed men seized the wagon with Duggan in it and drove to a cottonwood tree, where they hanged him. Dave Cook was furious when he learned that a disloyal employee had revealed his plan, and that this had resulted in a lynching, a practice he loathed.

There were no major crimes during Cook's third term as city marshal, and in 1869, he was nominated for sheriff of Arapaho County. He went to Chicago and several large midwestern cities to learn more about crime-fighting methods. He was elected Arapaho County sheriff and appointed captain of Company A, First Regiment of the Colorado Militia. In 1874, he was promoted to major general and served in the militia for ten years. He was also appointed deputy U.S. marshal, headquartered in Denver. In September 1875, Cook was elected to a second term as Arapaho County sheriff.

The detective association received appeals for help in solving crimes from all over the United States. Under Cook's direction, the organization helped track down and jail swindlers and gangs of thieves who were robbing freight trains. Information sharing by members helped solve several notorious murders and capture the culprits.

Cook's term as Arapaho County sheriff ended in 1879. By 1880, anti-Chinese sentiment had grown in Denver, although there was a very small Asian population of about 238. After a torchlight parade on election night, November 2, 1880, a mob began tearing up the Chinese Quarter in Denver. A lynch mob hanged an innocent old man and then began setting fires. The mayor called an emergency meeting with the police chief and city officials, who agreed they needed Dave Cook's help.

Cook responded quickly and assembled one hundred trusted men, who successfully broke up a mob of three thousand rioters. The leaders were arrested and jailed, and only one Asian was killed. When Denver's police chief resigned after this trouble, Cook took over and was elected to the job by a landslide. He served one year as police chief and resigned in 1881, despite pressure to remain. He served as deputy U.S. marshal for ten years and continued as head of the detective association. In 1882, Cook published his memoir, *Hands Up! or Thirty-Five Years of Detective Work in the Mountains and on the Plains.*

During the 1890s, Dave Cook was called to clean up Denver's corrupt city government. He ruthlessly exposed officials who'd made deals with the con man Soapy Smith that permitted him to continue his swindling activities. Denver's citizens were furious and swept the corrupt politicians out of office in the 1892 elections. Newly elected Governor Waite fired the entire Denver Police Department and offered Cook any law enforcement position he wanted. The lawman agreed to organize and supervise a detective department for the Denver police. He remained in charge of this new department for the rest of his life, never retiring. Dave Cook continued doing the work he loved until he died on February 28, 2007.

Dave Cook was an excellent horseman, a crack shot, and a skilled outdoorsman, and he was absolutely fearless. He was over six feet tall, well-built, and able to handle himself in a fight. He had many friends and enjoyed playing cards, smoking cigars, telling jokes and stories, and having an occasional drink.

During his long career, Dave Cook arrested over three thousand criminals and more than fifty murderers. He helped organize more effective law enforcement through information sharing and mutual cooperation, eliminating the need for vigilance committees.

2

THE BLOODY ESPINOSAS

COLORADO'S FIRST SERIAL KILLERS

Spring had finally come to the southern Colorado Territory in 1863, but people didn't rush out to greet it—they stayed inside their homes, afraid. Prospectors cast fearful glances over their shoulders as they worked their mining claims, and teamsters were unwilling to venture out on the roads. They were reluctant to leave the protection of a town or a fort, and supplies grew scarce. There had been several mysterious murders in which the killer had struck quickly and left behind only a body and no clues. The bodies of the victims were often slashed and mutilated, and no one was left alive to describe the butcher. Who was the fiend murdering miners, travelers on lonely roads, and ranchers in their remote cabins? The fear of the unseen—of the unknown—cast a dark shadow over the vast area of South Park.

This story of murder and revenge began in San Rafael, a tiny village in a remote corner of the San Luis Valley, where Felipe and Vivián Espinosa settled with their families. They'd come from New Mexico looking for a better life, but they hadn't found it. Farming their little piece of land didn't produce enough to feed their wives and children, so they decided to steal horses and rob freight wagons.

In January 1863, they stopped a freight wagon loaded with goods for a New Mexico trading post that was operated by a priest. They emptied the wagon, loaded the plunder on their horses, and galloped off. The driver recognized the Espinosa brothers and told the priest, who was furious at being robbed. He reported the theft to General Carlton, the

South Park from Kenosha Pass. *Photograph by Tom Williams.*

territorial commander headquartered in Santa Fe. Carlton sent orders to Lieutenant Colonel Sam Tappan, the commanding officer at Fort Garland, to arrest the Espinosas.

Lieutenant Hodt and fifteen troopers, accompanied by U.S. Marshal George Austen went to the Espinosas' small adobe house. They decided the easiest way to capture the thieves was to lie and say they were recruiting for the army. Felipe was immediately suspicious, so he grabbed his gun and began shooting. The soldiers scattered, but a corporal was killed, and the Espinosas fled.

The soldiers searched the surrounding area, but they couldn't find the two men. So, they returned to loot the Espinosas' tiny house, taking all their food, clothing, blankets, pots and pans. They hauled everything to Fort Garland, where they claimed these items had been stolen by the Espinosa brothers. When Felipe and Vivián returned to their adobe, they found their families terrified and without food, clothing, blankets, or any of the basic things they needed to survive. They had little before, but now, they had nothing. Furious, Felipe vowed to take revenge on every Anglo (white person) in the Colorado Territory. In early March 1863, he and Vivián headed toward Canon City, where they began their murderous rampage against all Anglos. Their bloody vendetta would deliver death to at least thirty-two innocent people.

Franklin Bruce was the first to die. He'd brought his family west in 1860, and they had a small farm on Hardscrabble Creek in the foothills of the Wet Mountains. On March 16, 1863, he was at work, building a sawmill on the creek, when the Espinosa brothers suddenly appeared and shot him in the heart. Felipe whipped out his bowie knife and slashed a large cross across the dead man's chest. The brothers tore apart the sawmill and then got on their horses and rode north.

Henry Harkins and three friends prospected at Buckskin Joe but didn't find much gold, so they decided to return to farming. Harkins was building a sawmill so he could process logs into planks and build frame houses. On March 18, Harkins stopped work and headed for his cabin to get supper ready for his hungry friends. Later, when they walked up to the cabin, they found Harkins sprawled in the doorway, dead with a bullet hole in his forehead. His skull had been split into pieces with a hatchet, and he'd been stabbed twice in the left side of his chest. Horrified, Harkins's friends searched the area and found horse tracks leading away from the cabin. Shortly after, the sheriff and a deputy who were trailing the murderer of William Bruce rode up. They speculated that Harkins and Bruce had been killed by the same person and quickly rode off, following the tracks that were heading west.

As news of the murders spread across South Park, fear gripped everyone. Nothing happened for thirteen days, and then the body of John Addelman, a hay farmer, was found near his cabin in a remote corner of South Park. He had been shot and robbed.

On April 7, Jacob Binkley and Abram Shoup loaded their picks and shovels into a wagon, hitched up their oxen, and left Buckskin Joe. They were headed for the new gold strikes in Montana, and after traveling about ninety miles, they reached Kenosha Pass. Their oxen climbed the gradual incline, and when they reached the top, they made camp in a shallow arroyo. Travelers passing by on the road to Denver saw them cooking their supper as darkness fell.

The next morning, the owner of the nearby stage station, the Kenosha House, found the young prospectors' oxen wandering about loose. The animals were rounded up and driven to the prospectors' camp, which had been ransacked. Worried, the men from the stage station searched the area and found Binkley's body lying face down in the brush. He'd been shot in the chest and robbed. About four hundred yards away, they discovered Shoup's corpse crumpled in a gulch. He had several stab wounds in his chest, but he had managed to run away from his attacker before he collapsed and died.

Henry Harkins's grave site, near Fort Carson, Colorado. *Photograph by C. Hatch, 2013.*

As the body count rose, there was growing panic in South Park, and every stranger became a suspect. Rumors were rampant, as some speculated that Ute Indians were the killers; others thought a gang of ruthless outlaws was responsible. Some theorized that the terrorists were vicious Confederate guerrillas from Texas. South Park was a perfect killing ground for the Espinosas. This remote alpine valley is ringed by mountains and encompasses over one thousand square miles. To the west are the mountains and mining camps of Buckskin Joe, California Gulch, and Leadville; while Fairplay sits at the base of the northern mountains. The road to Denver runs east over Kenosha Pass, and to the south lies the Arkansas River Valley.

On April 15, 1863, Governor Evans, along with the territorial legislature and relatives of the victims, offered a reward of $2,500 for the capture of the killer. Fear of the mysterious murderer increased the tension felt throughout the Colorado Territory as the Civil War raged on. There were many Southern sympathizers in the mining camps, but Union sentiment was strong in Denver and the northern part of the Colorado Territory. Two companies of experienced Colorado volunteers scoured South Park, certain the killers were Confederates, but they found nothing to substantiate this.

Around the first week in May, Bill Carter, a young prospector, and two miner friends purchased lumber at the Montgomery sawmill and began loading it in their wagon. Bill worked for a while but decided he didn't want to wait until his companions finished the job and were ready to return to Fairplay with the load of lumber. He elected to walk several miles back to town, even though it was already dusk. Carter's friends urged him to wait and reminded him of the recent murders, but he ignored their warnings and set off.

It was nearly dark when Carter was surprised by two men on horseback. They appeared suddenly out of the shadowy forest, and without warning, the larger man pulled his revolver and shot Carter in the chest. The bullets killed him instantly, and the two men dragged his body off the road. They rifled his pockets, took his gun, and threw his body into a ditch. Then they disappeared into the darkness.

When Bill didn't show up in Fairplay that night, his friends organized a search party and headed up the road to Montgomery. They found Carter's body in the ditch with bullet wounds in his chest, and his head had been slashed and hacked. His body was taken to Fairplay by his brother, while the rest of the search party found the footprints of two men. They followed the tracks to the South Platte River, where the killers took to the water, obliterating their trail.

A period illustration depicting the murderous brothers Felipe and Vivián Espinosa in action. *Genealogy Images of History*.

On May 4, two days after Bill Carter was murdered, there was another attack. This time, the killers struck on Red Hill Pass, murdering Fred Lehman and Sol Seyga, two prospectors, returning from Denver. They were leading their horses up the steep road when Seyga suddenly slumped to the ground, dead. He had a gunshot wound in his chest. Then Lehman was shot in the arm, but he managed to draw his revolver and shoot at his attackers. He emptied his gun and then turned and started running, but he was shot in the back and crumpled to the ground.

Three other prospectors returning from Denver found the two dead men lying in the road. The clothes of both had been stripped off, and Lehman's head had been beaten and crushed with a rock. Their belongings and horses were gone, but a note was nailed to a nearby tree. Written in Spanish, it promised, "Vengeance to be taken on Anglos as a sacrifice to the Virgin."

There was no one alive who could describe the killers, and despite the violence of the murders, nothing had been left behind—there were no clues. As the body count rose, panic gripped southern Colorado. On May 4, Edward Metcalf drove a wagonload of lumber from the Montgomery sawmill to Fairplay. He picked up his mail at the post office and stuffed the thick packet of letters into the left breast pocket of his coat. Then he whipped up his team and started down the road. As he passed a large clump of bushes, a swarthy man stepped out and shot at him. The force of the bullet knocked him backward into the wagon, but the bullet was deflected away from his heart by the thick packet of mail. As the startled team bolted, Metcalf recovered, sat up and looked back. He saw two Mexican men standing in the bushes: one was aiming a rifle at him, while the other was reloading. Both men shot at him several times, but he was soon out of range.

The gunfire startled a man named Allen, who was staying at the Cottage Grove Roadhouse nearby. He grabbed his rifle and ran out to the road, where he saw two men shooting at Metcalf. He fired several shots at them. They whirled around and disappeared into the brush, but Allen had gotten a good look at them. Meantime, Metcalf whipped up his team and hurried on to Fairplay. When he reached town, he gasped out his story and described his assailants as "Negroes," and "men with blackened skin." He said one was large and dark, wearing a wide-brimmed white hat; the other was short and smaller. Allen gave a similar description of the two men he'd seen shooting at Metcalf.

Lehman and Seyga had been popular prospectors in California Gulch, and a posse was raised to look for the brutes who'd murdered them. Charles Carter, whose brother Bill had been murdered, joined them, and Captain John McCannon was elected their leader. This posse from California Gulch crossed the Mosquito Range into South Park, where a messenger met them with Metcalf's description of the killers.

A late spring snowstorm had left the ground soft and wet, making the tracks of the two killers easy to follow. Determined to catch them, the posse rode all day, and around twilight, they followed the trail into a small valley near Four Mile Creek. They smelled smoke from a campfire and found two horses tethered in a grassy meadow. Since no one was in sight, the posse split up, surrounded the meadow, and settled down to wait. When a large, burly Mexican man stepped out of the brush and moved toward the horses, Joseph Lamb, a posse member, took careful aim and fired. The man cried out and fell but managed to draw his pistol and return fire. A shotgun blast from the posse missed him but killed his horse. Then Charles Carter aimed carefully and pulled the trigger, hitting the man in the head. Suddenly, a smaller Mexican man dashed out of the trees and ran to his fallen companion. Seeing there was nothing he could do for him, he turned and disappeared into the bushes.

The posse searched the area, but the smaller man was gone. When they went through the killers' saddlebags, the posse found personal items and papers and even some pieces of clothing that belonged to the murdered men. Harkins's gold-framed spectacles were there, as was a small bag of gold dust, and a memoranda book that had been used. The entries, written in Spanish, were angry rants against white Americans, and boasted that they'd killed thirty-two men already and threatened to "exterminate whites as revenge for infamies committed against our families." The writer promised that "we are going down to the plains to kill more." The name Espinosa was written in the memoranda book, leaving little doubt that these two men were the Espinosa brothers of Conejos. The posse determined the dead man was Vivián; while Felipe had escaped.

It's believed that the posse cut off Vivián's head, and that a well-known doctor kept his bleached skull for years. Vivián's rifle went to a private collector. After another futile search of the valley, the posse left Vivián's body where it lay and returned to California Gulch. They received a heroes' welcome, and the *Weekly Commonwealth* of May 21, 1863, trumpeted, "Glorious News! Mysterious Murders Unraveled at Last! The Principal Murderer Shot!" The *Rocky Mountain News Weekly* identified the Espinosa brothers as the killers who'd committed at least a dozen murders. The newspapers quickly came up with a name for the two: the "Bloody Espinosas."

Felipe Espinosa had escaped from the posse with only his rifle, a revolver, and the clothes he was wearing. Without a horse, food, or blankets, he trudged over 150 miles of rugged mountains to reach his home. He dropped out of sight, and many thought he'd fled to Mexico. There were no killings for several months, and everyone breathed a sigh of relief.

Late that summer, Felipe retraced his steps to the campsite near Four Mile Creek, found and buried his brother's remains. He returned home with a macabre reminder of Vivián: his shrunken, dried foot. Felipe vowed the Anglos would pay for killing Vivián and causing all his family's misfortunes. He recruited his nephew, sixteen-year-old José Vincente Espinosa, to be his killing partner and made plans to resume his slaughter of Anglos.

The next victim was William Smith, who'd made the unfortunate decision to go fishing in the Conejos River near the Espinosa adobe. Leon Constantine, a young French Canadian farmer and trader, was murdered near Huerfano Butte in September 1863. In October, the Espinosas camped near Sangre de Cristo Pass, where they planned to ambush every Anglo traveler who came by. On October 10, they attacked Leander Philbrook and Dolores Sanchez, who were traveling in a buggy to Costilla. When the Espinosas stopped them, they jumped out of the buggy and ran up the rocky canyon. Philbrook escaped and managed to cross twelve miles of rough country in the dark to reach Fort Garland. Dolores hid in the boulders while the Espinosas ransacked their luggage, burned the buggy, and then rode away.

A wagon finally approached, and Dolores ran out of her hiding place to stop it. After hearing her story, the driver hid her under blankets in his wagon and started for the fort. Farther down the road, he was stopped by the Espinosas, who found Dolores while searching the wagon for plunder. They dragged her out of the wagon, forced the driver to leave, assaulted her, and then tied her up and left her lying in the brush by the road. Dolores managed to get out of her bonds and was hurrying down the road when a group of soldiers found her and took her to Fort Garland.

Fort Garland Parade Field, where soldiers presented themselves for inspection and practiced marching and close-order drills. *Photograph by Tom Williams.*

Pistols, now in the History Colorado Center's collection, allegedly used by the Espinosa brothers. *A. Marcus, 1970; History Colorado.*

Determined to end the Espinosa rampage, Colonel Tappan sent a courier to Tom Tobin at his Trinchera ranch. The scout wasted no time getting to Fort Garland and quickly agreed to hunt down the killers and bring them in. On October 12, after midnight, Tobin, Lieutenant Colonel Baldwin, fifteen troopers, and a boy to handle the scout's horse left Fort Garland to find the Espinosas.

Tobin was sure the killers were hiding near Sangre de Cristo Pass, where they could ambush travelers on the road to the fort. The posse rode all night and reached the area at daylight, and they immediately began looking for the killers' footprints. Tobin and four soldiers spent the next three days scrambling up steep slopes and struggling through dense brush around the pass. Lieutenant Colonel Baldwin and the troopers blocked the canyon's entrance preventing the Espinosas' escape.

On the fourth morning of their search, Tobin and his team found the tracks of two men and followed their trail. The undergrowth became so thick, they had to crawl, and they tried to avoid loose rocks and twigs to be as quiet as possible. Tobin spotted the Espinosas' camp just ahead, signaled the soldiers to a halt, and whispered. "Cock yer guns….Hold yer fire till I say."

He inched forward, his long rifle ready, until he could see the back of Felipe's head. The killer whirled around, saw Tobin and lunged for his gun. Tobin pulled the trigger and shot Felipe in the chest, knocking him down. Felipe screamed to José, "Run, run! I am killed!" Tobin yelled, "Shoot, boys!" José ran out of a nearby ravine and raced toward a grove of aspen. The troopers fired at him but missed. Tobin took aim, pulled the trigger and hit José, killing him instantly.

Felipe Espinosa was still alive and crawled to a tree, where he managed to sit up and take a shot at the troopers. He missed, and they riddled him with bullets. Tobin pulled out his big knife, grabbed Espinosa by the hair and cut off his head. Next José's body was decapitated, and the two heads were stuffed in a flour sack. They were carried back to Fort Garland and presented to Major Tappan, closing one of the most violent chapters in Colorado's history.

Author's note: The heads were displayed at Fort Garland for a while, but it's uncertain where they ended up. There were rumors that they were stored in the basement of the capitol building or tucked away by the Colorado Historical Society. Tom Tobin never received the $2,500 reward for killing the Espinosas.

3

TOM TOBIN ENDS A BLOODY RAMPAGE

Tom Tobin was the tough frontiersman who ended the bloody rampage of Colorado's first serial killers, the Espinosas. Felipe Espinosa, his brother Vivián, and nephew José Vincente are believed to have murdered at least thirty-two people in 1863.

In 1837, when he was fourteen, Tom Tobin left his French Canadian mulatto mother and sister in St. Louis and joined his older half-brother, Charles Autobees, in New Mexico. He discarded his surname, Tobin, and adopted his brother's name, Autobees, which he used for the next fifteen years. Charley and Tom worked for Simon Turley, who was building a trading post, gristmill, and distillery at Arroyo Hondo, nine miles from Taos on the Taos Trail. Tom led pack trains loaded with barrels of Turley's Taos Lightning to Santa Fe and north to Forts Vasquez and Lupton in Colorado. He exchanged the potent whiskey for beaver pelts and buffalo hides, which he sold in St. Louis on his annual spring trip. He used that money to buy supplies and merchandise for Turley's trading post.

When Tom was twenty-one, he bought a Hawken rifle, a powerful black powder muzzle loader, and became a crack shot. In addition to acquiring a fine gun, Tom acquired a young wife, fifteen-year-old Pasquala Bernal. Her mother gave the newlyweds a piece of land with a small adobe cottage. Tom and Charley joined the Catholic Church, became naturalized Mexican citizens, and enjoyed a pleasant life raising their young families. This all vanished when tensions between Mexico and the United States exploded into the Mexican-American War in May 1846.

Thomas Tate Tobin, American adventurer, tracker, trapper, mountain man, guide, U.S. Army scout and occasional bounty hunter. *Public domain.*

General Kearney's troops marched into Santa Fe in August 1846 and seized control of the region. Mexican citizens and Puebloans resented the invasion by the Americans and plotted a revolt. In the early hours of January 19, 1847, a mob of Native Americans and Mexicans broke into the home of Charles Bent, the first territorial governor. They killed and scalped him in front of his family and then rushed to Sheriff Stephen Lee's home and murdered him. Next, the mob scalped District Attorney Leal while he was still alive and threw him into a ditch.

The following morning, the insurgents surrounded Turley's trading post and demanded that he and his eight American employees surrender. Turley, Tom Tobin, and the others refused, and immediately, the mob began shooting, filling the air with whizzing bullets and arrows. The battle began at dawn but was lost by dusk, when the mob broke through the post's adobe walls and set the building on fire. Tom and Johnny Albert, the only survivors, cut holes in a rear wall of the post and escaped into the darkness.

Albert made his way north to safety at El Pueblo in Colorado, while Tom fled to Santa Fe. Tom located his brother, and they were among the first to sign up with Ceran St. Vrain's company of volunteers, all experienced frontiersmen. They became part of Colonel Sterling Price's small army of 285 men determined to defeat the rebels, retake Taos, and restore peace to northern New Mexico.

On January 20, the same day Turley's post was destroyed, the insurgents killed eight American traders at the small village of Mora. Two days later, about 150 rebels attacked a smaller unit of Americans and killed their leader, Captain Israel Hendley, in the First Battle of Mora. On January 23, 1847, Tobin and Charley were part of Colonel Price's troops that routed a combined force of 1,500 Mexicans and Puebloans at the village of Santa Cruz de la Cañada. Next, they defeated over 700 rebels at Embudo. On February 1, American forces destroyed the village of Mora and killed every rebel who didn't surrender.

After struggling through deep snow and bitter cold, they reached Taos on February 3. About 600 men had taken refuge in San Geronimo de Taos, a large church built in 1610, ten years before the Mayflower landed. The church had adobe walls that were three feet thick with narrow openings for rifles. After two days of fighting, Price's men used axes to chop holes through the adobe walls so their howitzers could fire inside the church. The destruction was terrible.

Tobin and several volunteers stormed the church and found that all the rebels had been killed by the cannon fire, and the building was in ruins. This ended the 1847 Taos Revolt, a tragic part of the war between Mexico and the United States. In the 1848 Treaty of Guadalupe Hidalgo, Mexico ceded 55 percent of its territory to the United States, including the present-day states of California, Nevada, Utah, New Mexico, most of Arizona and

Colorado, and parts of Oklahoma, Kansas, and Wyoming. It gave up all claim to Texas and recognized the Rio Grande as the southern border of the United States.

Turley was dead; his trading post was destroyed, and the leaders of the revolt were hanged. Tom and Charley decided to leave Arroyo Hondo and build a new life for their families in Colorado. They began farming near the St. Charles River, east of Pueblo, and sold their record crops in Taos and Bent's Fort that fall. The following year, Charley returned to farming, while Tom became an army scout for Colonel Gilpin and spent several months searching for the winter camps of Cheyenne and Arapaho on the plains.

In 1852, Tom was hired to guide Lieutenant Edwin Beale's expedition to locate a railroad route from St. Louis to California. Pleased to have Tobin as a scout, Beale described the frontiersman as "having a reputation almost equal to Kit Carson's for bravery, dexterity with his rifle, and skill in mountain life." They traveled west on the Old Spanish Trail, across the deserts of Arizona and California, and suffered terribly in the summer heat. Despite these challenges, they found a railroad route, and Tobin led

Ruins of the San Geronimo de Taos Mission and Taos Pueblo Cemetery, 2019. *Photograph by Tom Williams.*

the triumphant expedition into Los Angeles on August 22, 1853. After this experience, Lieutenant Beale's campaign to use camels for desert travel was successful.

By 1852, large numbers of Hispanic families from New Mexico had settled in the San Luis Valley, and Fort Massachusetts had been built to protect them from the Utes. A new fort was under construction in 1856, and Charley supervised the production of adobe bricks. He was stabbed and seriously injured in an argument with a worker, so Tom took over and work continued. The new fort, which was comprised of twenty-two adobe buildings, was completed in 1858. It was named Fort Garland after General George Garland, commander of the Military District of New Mexico.

In May 1856, Tom bought a parcel of land in Costilla, built an adobe house and barn, and moved his family from Arroyo Hondo to their new home in Colorado. Since he was a veteran of the Mexican-American War, he petitioned for 160 acres of land on Trinchera Creek, near Fort Garland. He planned to raise cattle, horses, and produce to sell to the army.

In 1859, three years after Tom applied, his request for the Trinchera Creek land was approved, and his future looked bright. The 1860 census listed his personal property worth $3,000, and his real estate was worth $2,000. He was selling bumper crops of vegetables and hay to Fort Garland, and his horse business was growing. The Civil War was on the horizon in 1861, and there were many Southern supporters in the newly created Colorado Territory. Neither Charley nor Tom took sides and tried to carry on as usual.

Lieutenant Colonel Samuel Tappan, First Colorado Regiment of Volunteers. *Library of Congress, https://loc.gov/pictures/resource/cwpb.05798/.*

In 1863, a series of bloody murders overshadowed Civil War news, and people in southern Colorado were terrified. The first killing occurred in March 1863 in the foothills of the Wet Mountains. Franklin Bruce was building a sawmill on Hardscrabble Creek when he was attacked and killed. His murder was followed in rapid succession by the killing of Henry Harkins northeast of Canon City, and then John Addleman was shot to death in South Park. On April 8, 1863, two prospectors, Jacob

Binkley and Abram Shoupe, were murdered near Kenosha Pass. Then Bill Carter, a young prospector, was killed on May 2 on the road to Fairplay. On May 4, Fred Lehman and Sol Seyga, miners from California Gulch, were shot and killed as they walked up Red Hill Pass in South Park.

All the victims had fatal bullet wounds, and the bodies of some were slashed with a knife. The heads of others were hacked or chopped with an axe or hatchet. The *Rocky Mountain News* of May 7, 1863, wrote, "All, from the beginning have been marked with a peculiar singularity of the most fiendish and diabolical atrocity."

No one lived to describe their attacker, and despite the violence of the murders, no clues were left behind. As the body count rose, panic gripped much of the territory. The February 11, 1872 issue of the *Rocky Mountain News* described that terrifying time:

> *The people were appalled, stricken with fear, scarcely daring to venture beyond the reach of immediate aid.…No one could tell from what concealment the messenger of death which had never missed his mark might reach him. The dread, despair, feeling of uncertainty, the reign of terror, the fear of the unseen, and unknown foe pervaded the hearts of those sturdy pioneers who dared face any danger, open and known.*

In May, Edwin Metcalf was attacked but escaped and described his assailants. The posse that searched South Park found their tracks and followed the killers to their camp. There was a gunfight, and one murderer, identified as Vivián Espinosa, was killed, but his brother, Felipe, escaped and dropped out of sight for several months. There were no more killings until September 1863, when Bill Smith was murdered while fishing in the Conejos River. Then Leon Constantine was killed near Huerfano Butte. When Colonel Sam Tappan took over the command of Fort Garland on July 1, 1863, Governor Evans said that his immediate assignment was to "hunt down and kill or capture the bandit, Felipe Espinosa."

On October 10, 1863, Leander Philbrook and Dolores Sanchez, who were traveling by buggy to the settlement of Costilla, were attacked and robbed by the Espinosas. Philbrook jumped out of the buggy and escaped, but Dolores Sanchez was assaulted by the killers. Then they tied her up and left her lying in the brush near the road. She got out of her bonds and was rescued by soldiers who took her to Fort Garland. Meanwhile, Philbrook trudged twelve miles across rugged country to the fort, where he and Dolores identified the Espinosas as their attackers.

After hearing their stories, Colonel Tappan sent a courier to Tom Tobin at his Trinchera ranch. He knew the mountain man was a lifelong friend of Kit Carson, who had often said Tobin could "track a grasshopper through sagebrush." Tappan asked him to come immediately "prepared for a trip into the mountains." Tobin packed his gear and headed for Fort Garland.

Determined to stop the Espinosas' deadly rampage, Colonel Tappan asked Tobin to hunt down the killers and bring them in—he promised he would be rewarded. The scout wanted to go after the killers alone, but Tappan insisted that a few soldiers accompany him. An expert tracker, Tobin knew he would be on foot most of the time, so he asked for Juan Montoya, fourteen years old, to be responsible for his horse. So, after midnight on October 12, Tobin, Lieutenant Baldwin, fifteen troopers, and Montoya left Fort Garland.

The road to Fort Garland passed through Sangre de Cristo Canyon, where Tobin believed the Espinosas would lie in wait to ambush travelers. The group rode all night and reached the canyon around dawn. They decided Tobin and four soldiers would work their way up the canyon to look for the fugitives' tracks. Lieutenant Baldwin and the others remained in the lower canyon to block the Espinosas' escape.

They spent three days scrambling up steep slopes, fighting their way through dense underbrush, always alert for any sign the killers were near. On the fourth morning, they found the footprints of the two men and followed them to their camp. Tobin shot and wounded Felipe, who was then killed by the soldiers. Then Tobin killed José as he ran from the camp. Their heads were collected and stuffed in a sack to be taken to Fort Garland.

The soldiers searched the Espinosas' camp, collecting rifles, pistols, butcher knives, and the stolen baggage and clothing of Sanchez and Philbrook. There was an unfinished letter from Felipe to Governor Evans that demanded land and a pardon and threatened to kill six hundred additional Anglos if the pardon was denied "because…in killing one gains his liberty."

The Espinosas' bodies were left where they fell, and Tobin and his men rode down the canyon to meet Lieutenant Baldwin and the troopers. They returned to Fort Garland on October 16 and went to Colonel Tappan's office. Tobin said, "I have got them." Then he took the heads out of the sack and set them on the floor. Lieutenant Baldwin confirmed the identity of the gruesome souvenirs and added, "There is no mistake, for we have this diary and papers and letters to show that they were the assassins." Tappan told Tobin that the *Rocky Mountain News* had announced a $2,500 reward for the capture of the murderers, and he urged him to apply. Tom replied that he

Tobin in his later years. *Public domain.*

hadn't hunted down the Espinosas for money—he thought it was his duty as a citizen.

Colonel Tappan issued a congratulatory order to the troops, and everyone in the territory was thankful that the killers were dead and that their year of terror was over. Tobin returned to his ranch, where he and his wife, Pasquala, raised six children and adopted a young Native American girl. In 1882, Charley Autobees died from a lingering infection that set in after he accidentally shot himself. In 1887, Tobin was devastated when his wife, Pasquala, died suddenly at the age of fifty-seven. He fell into a deep depression, neglected the ranch and stock, and spent hours sitting at Pasquala's grave. When he was sixty-four, he married Rosa Quintana, the forty-year-old widow of a friend.

Tobin's daughter, Pasqualita, later married Billy Carson, the son of the scout Kit Carson. In May 1888, in a drunken rage, Billy beat Pasqualita, and she fled home to her father. Tobin was infuriated and raced into town, where he tried unsuccessfully to stab his son-in-law. Then he pulled his revolver and shot at Billy, who returned fire, critically wounding Tobin. The doctor was summoned and delivered the grim news that Tom Tobin was probably going to die from his wounds.

Billy Carson was arrested and thrown in jail, while Tobin remained in critical condition for several weeks. *The Independent Journal* of May 24, 1888, reported, "Thomas Tate Tobin…is slightly improving. All odds of him pulling through were given up at first but owing to the wonderful condition of the old man he may possibly get well." Tom never fully recovered, but he outlived Billy Carson, who accidentally shot himself in the leg on January 18, 1889. The wound wasn't serious, but Carson died of lockjaw within twelve hours.

Tom walked with a cane, but he wasn't able to do the strenuous work needed to run the ranch. As his financial situation worsened, he tried, unsuccessfully, to collect the $2,500 reward for killing the Espinosas. He sold the stock from his ranch, but that money didn't last, and he was soon living in poverty. Learning of his dire financial condition, Colorado Senator B. Smith, a longtime admirer of the old scout, managed to get a bill passed by the General Assembly that awarded Tobin $1,000 for killing the Espinosas.

This money helped, and in 1896, Tobin applied for his share of a newly appropriated fund that would be used pay veterans of St. Vrain's Company who fought in the 1847 Taos Revolt. That fund quickly ran out of money before Tom could collect his share of a few hundred dollars. In poverty once again, he applied for the government pension of eight

Above: Tom Tobin's Colt revolver. Folklore says Major W.M. Dunn gifted this revolver to Tom in 1883 at Fort Garland as a thank-you for all the work he had done for the government. *Photograph by N. McClure, 2003; Buffalo Bill Center of the West Firearms Museum.*

Left: Tom Tobin's grave site, MacMullen Cemetery, Blanca, Colorado. *Photograph by D. Dolton, 2023.*

dollars a month for his military service in the Taos Revolt. His request was rejected because there was no record that showed St. Vrain's Company was ever mustered into U.S. service. The uprising had been squashed so quickly that the troops never served the thirty days required for a pension. Next, Tobin requested this pension with the help of both Colorado state senators, but he was rejected again. Then a U.S. senator tried to get a bill through Congress to grant a pension to all of St. Vrain's veterans. Requests for this pension went to the secretary of war and the U.S. Army, but each one was rejected due to various technicalities.

As his financial situation became more desperate, Tobin sold his last parcel of land, along with his house, to a friend—with the provision that he could live there the rest of his life. When Tobin died, his friend was also to provide a casket and suit for his burial. Since Tobin had no cash, he obtained food on credit at a friend's grocery. He never received the $2,500 reward offered by Governor Evans for killing the Espinosas.

In 1899, Tobin's son Tom Jr., a prison guard at the state penitentiary, was killed during an escape attempt. The depressed old man's fragile health worsened, and on May 15, 1904, Tom Tobin died. He was buried next to his wife, Pasquala, in the small MacMullin Cemetery on the privately owned Blanca Trinchera Ranch, Costilla County, Colorado.

4

WILLIE KENNARD CLEANS UP YANKEE HILL

Willie Kennard was a fighting man. He had years of experience to back up his claim that he was the right man for the job of marshal of Yankee Hill. This bustling gold mining camp had been in the grip of Barney Casewit, a vicious outlaw, for over two years. Casewit had cheated, bullied, and terrorized citizens ever since he came to town, and he didn't hesitate to kill anyone brave enough to stand up to him.

The miners living in small cabins scattered across the windswept slopes of Yankee Hill wanted their families to be safe. They were horrified when Casewit pounced on fifteen-year-old Birdie Campbell, raped and strangled her, and tossed her body into the bushes. Her father, a well-liked bookkeeper at the bank, went gunning for Casewit and was shot for his trouble. When Yankee Hill's Marshal Craig tried to arrest him for the crime, Casewit quickly pulled his six-shooter and killed him.

The mayor and town council hired another lawman, a man named Reed, but he, too, ended up at the undertaker after confronting Casewit. The last man who'd signed up to enforce the law in Yankee Hill quietly turned in his badge and slipped out of town after seeing Casewit gun down two cowboys.

Angry citizens were up in arms and demanded that this deadly killer be stopped. Desperate for help, the town council placed an advertisement for a marshal in the *Rocky Mountain News* in the summer of 1874. The job paid $100 a month—good pay in those days—and Willie Kennard decided to apply. He arrived in Yankee Hill and found Mayor Matt Borden and the city councilmen enjoying their morning coffee at the café. The tall Black

Placer gold mining at Gregory Gulch. *History Colorado.*

man approached their table and announced that he'd seen the newspaper advertisement and was applying for the job of city marshal. To say the mayor and city council were surprised is an understatement. Ignoring Kennard's revolvers, one on each hip, a member challenged, "You mean you could read that newspaper ad, boy?" A scornful glance was Kennard's only answer. Years later, councilman and lawyer Bert Corgan wrote in his memoir, *Mining Camp Lawyer*, "I was perplexed by this darky. He was either, I calculated, an impetuous bunghead or as cold-blooded a gunslinger as ever I saw. "

Confronting the council's obvious doubt and suspicion, Willie Kennard told them just who he was and why he was qualified to become the tough marshal Yankee Hill desperately needed. Willie was born around 1832, and when the Civil War began, he joined Illinois's Twenty-Ninth United States Colored Infantry, a regiment of the United States Colored Troops who were part of the Union army.

He'd fought at the Battles of Antietam and Gettysburg and had taken part in the Carolina Campaign. When the Civil War ended, Kennard enlisted in the Ninth Cavalry Buffalo Soldiers and went to Fort Bliss, Texas, where he fought Comanches. At Fort Davis, he was a firearms instructor who taught Black men—who were formerly enslaved and forbidden to touch guns—how to shoot. He was with the Buffalo Soldiers who fought the Mescalero Apaches in the Guadelupe Mountains of West Texas. Kennard served in the Southwest with the Buffalo Soldiers for many years and was about forty-two years old when he arrived in Yankee Hill.

It was obvious to Mayor Borden that Kennard was a tough man, and he said the job was his if he could arrest that notorious criminal Barney Casewit. The council agreed but warned Kennard that Casewit had killed several lawmen and citizens. They were impressed by Kennard when the mayor handed him the marshal's badge, and he coolly pinned it on.

Kennard headed for the saloon where Casewit was playing poker with his sidekicks. Mayor Borden and the city council trailed along behind at a safe distance. Kennard walked in the door of the saloon, stopped to survey the room, and carefully sized up Casewit and his cronies. Then he walked over to their poker table and said clearly, "Barney Casewit, you're under arrest."

The outlaw glanced up at the tall Black man and sneered, "Oh yeah—you think I'm comin' with you? Where're we goin'?" As his poker-playing buddies laughed hilariously, Kennard replied quietly, "It's your choice—to jail or to hell."

Casewit jumped to his feet and grabbed for his guns. Faster than the eye could see, Kinnard drew his six-shooters and fired; his bullets hit the butts of Casewit's revolvers, ripping them from his hands and rendering them useless. Then the outlaw's henchmen, Ira Goodrich and Sam Betts, reached for their six-shooters, but Kennard dropped them both before their weapons even cleared leather.

"Hold on! Hold on!" Casewit shouted as his hands shot up in the air. He was taking no more chances with this Black gunslinger. The new marshal of Yankee Hill shoved a revolver into Casewit's back and marched him off to jail. There was no doubt in anyone's mind that Willie Kennard could handle this job.

The next morning, court was convened, with lawyer Bert Corgan, the only man who had any knowledge of the law, acting as judge. The court was called to order, and the facts were presented. Barney Casewit had a fair trial and was found guilty of rape and murder and sentenced to hang. In the interest of swift justice and the city's budget, Judge Corgan said money and time shouldn't be wasted building a gallows. He said Marshal Kennard should just nail a crossbar to a pine tree behind the blacksmith shop and carry out the sentence. This was done quickly.

After seeing Marshal Kennard in action, local miners, businessmen, gamblers, and townsfolk were certain he could keep order while they

An abandoned tubular steam boiler in the Leadville Mining District. *Photograph by Tom Williams.*

continued their search for gold. Some of them had come west in 1859 with the thousands of others who'd raced to the Colorado Territory shouting, "Pikes Peak or bust!" Prospectors had scrambled over canyons and through gulches to dig their glory holes and pan for gold in the icy streams. Hundreds of mining camps had been established by 1860, and more than ten thousand prospectors had crowded into the "richest square mile on Earth" around Central City.

Prospectors who didn't strike it rich at Black Hawk or who couldn't find a place to stake their claim around Central City drifted west to the steep hills near the Continental Divide. The pro-Union miners called this sprawling camp Yankee Hill. Its crude log cabins were scattered across the steep, west-facing slope of the "hill," which was ten thousand feet above sea level. There wasn't a main street or a town center, and it was windswept and frigid in the winter. Residents shivered in the cold blasts that blew off the glacier on a nearby mountain, and blizzards often howled around the flimsy cabins and boardinghouses.

By 1874, the camp was prospering, and there were several hundred permanent residents, plus a few hundred transient prospectors. Rooms at the boardinghouse were always full. It was an important stage stop on the road from Central City to Georgetown. Two stage lines ran through town. The Wells Fargo and Butterfield, Leavenworth & Holladay Stage and Mail Routes provided service six days a week from Idaho Springs to Yankee Hill. The Central City–Wells Fargo Stage ran from Central City, through Yankee Hill to Georgetown. Mining companies shipped ore on both over the Gold Trail Toll Road to Idaho Springs for processing in the mill.

Yankee Hill attracted men like Barney Casewit, who were fast with a gun and lacked a conscience. The criminal element was slowly taking over

Main Street, Central City. *H. Faul, 1862; Denver Public Library Special Collections [X-2659].*

before Willie Kennard came to town. Ridding the place of Casewit earned Kennard the respect of the citizens of Yankee Hill. Unfortunately, Reese Durham, the local manager of the Butterfield Stage Station, who was a resentful Southerner, would not accept a Black man as the town marshal. He questioned Kennard's ability to handle the demands of the job and his authority to arrest a white citizen. He growled that the phony lawman should be run out of town. One evening, after several shots of whiskey, Durham challenged Kennard to an old-fashioned gunfight and earned himself a permanent place in the cemetery.

In the spring of 1875, a gang of robbers started holding up freight wagons and stealing the gold shipments from the mines. They often stopped stagecoaches on lonely mountain roads, pilfered the express boxes, and robbed the passengers. There were eight outlaws in this gang led by Billy McGeorge, who'd recently escaped from the Colorado Territorial Prison at Canon City. The gang waylaid the Stalcup family as they traveled west from Ohio. The outlaws unhitched the family's team from their wagon, rummaged through their belongings, and took clothes and valuables. Then they killed the entire family and left their bodies lying in the road.

The citizens of Yankee Hill were furious about this terrible crime and anxious for Marshal Kennard to capture the killers. After the Stalcup family was buried, Kennard made his plans. He wisely decided that chasing eight outlaws through the rugged mountains wasn't the best way to capture them. So, he decided to set a trap. He had "wanted" posters made offering a fifty-dollar a reward for the capture of "Billy McGeorge, dead or alive." Then he plastered the area with these posters, nailing them to trees along the trails, pinning them on the walls of saloons and gambling halls, restaurants, boardinghouses, livery stables, and the mercantile.

When McGeorge first saw the poster nailed to a tree, he flew into a rage and ripped it down, yelling, "What is this lousy reward? Every other sheriff in this territory is offering a reward of at least $300!" Such a small reward was an insult. Wasn't he a dangerous outlaw? Seeing these posters everywhere infuriated McGeorge, and when other outlaws made jokes about the puny reward, he became angrier. The disgruntled outlaw and his gang headed for Yankee Hill, where they intended to "show that marshal a thing or two!" On June 28, 1875, McGeorge and his gang galloped boldly into Yankee Hill. Marshal Kennard had been alerted and was waiting for them. Standing on Main Street, his double-barreled shotgun loaded with buckshot, Kennard ordered, "Drop your guns, boys!" Cash Downing, McGeorge's right-hand man, and another outlaw behind him foolishly reached for their guns, but the marshal opened up with his shotgun. The blast blew Downing and his pal right out of their saddles and into eternity. Kennard growled, "Reach for the sky!" His eyes were fastened on McGeorge, and the shotgun was aimed at his chest. The outlaws dropped their guns and raised their hands into the air. As Kennard marched them off to jail, McGeorge swore that he'd get even, but that day would never come.

The following morning, lawyer Bert Corgan once again presided as the judge and called the court to order. The numerous charges against McGeorge and his gang were reviewed. McGeorge was tried for ordering the cold-blooded murders of the Stalcup family, as well as numerous holdups and robberies. He was found guilty. The rest of the gang were tried on robbery charges and sentenced to spend years behind the granite walls of the Colorado Territorial Prison. Judge Corgan sentenced Billy McGeorge to be hung from that same pine tree used to send Barney Casewit into the hereafter. Justice was swift, and Marshal Kennard carried out the sentence.

The citizens of Yankee Hill were grateful for the law and order that Marshal Kennard established and maintained in their town. By 1877,

Ruins of one of the few remaining log cabin structures on Yankee Hill. *Photograph by Tom Williams.*

Colorado's first Black lawman had decided to turn in his badge and move on. He said he was going east "to find a wife," but it's not known if his quest to find romance was successful. By 1884, he'd returned to Denver and was working as a bodyguard for Barney Ford, a formerly enslaved and prominent businessman who became known as the "Black Baron of Colorado." Willie Kennard's whereabouts or activities after that remain a mystery.

Today, Yankee Hill is gone and all but forgotten. Cold winds blow across the high hillsides that are covered in tree stumps, abandoned glory holes, the remnants of tumbled-down log cabins, and a maze of old trails.

5

THE REYNOLDS GANG

CONFEDERATES IN COLORADO

It was a terrible sight! Four dead bodies shackled and tied to trees. There was no sign of a fifth man—although Uncle Dick Wooten knew that five men of the Reynolds Gang were alive when they left the Denver Jail on or about September 1, 1864. They were guarded by a platoon of the Third Colorado Cavalry, commanded by Captain Theodore Cree. They were meant to be escorted to Fort Lyon and then transferred to Fort Leavenworth for a military trial.

There are conflicting accounts about the discovery of the bodies of the members of the Reynolds Gang. Some historians credit "Uncle Dick" Wooten, a frontiersman and prominent businessman who'd built the toll road over Raton Pass. A Southern sympathizer, Wooten knew the prisoners were Confederate guerrillas who were expected at Fort Lyon. When they didn't arrive, he started looking for them. He was outraged when he discovered the grisly scene near Russellville, about thirty miles south of Denver. On September 9, 1864, the *Rocky Mountain News* broke the official story that the end of the Reynolds Gang was caused by their "failed escape attempt." The paper reported that when the soldiers stopped to water their horses, "the prisoners made a concerted attempt to escape and they were fired upon by the guard, and all instantly killed."

This story was questioned immediately: Why would the prisoners attempt to escape when they were shackled and chained to trees? Public outrage increased when U.S. Attorney General S.E. Browne declared this was "a most foul murder carried out on the express orders of Colonel John Chivington."

Yet despite questions and accusations, many history books still claim that the Reynolds Gang was a band of disreputable robbers, murderers, and rapists. Newly discovered documents tell a very different story. The Reynolds Gang was a band of Confederate soldiers from Company A, Wells Battalion, Third Texas Cavalry. They were following the orders of Confederate General Douglas Cooper.

In 1861, the Colorado Territory was full of partisan tension long before the first shots of the Civil War were fired at Fort Sumter. About 40 percent of the prospectors who'd headed west in the 1859 Pikes Peak Gold Rush were from the South. There was a lot of support for the Confederacy throughout the mining camps, especially those in South Park. When the Civil War started, many Rebel sympathizers threw aside their picks and shovels and abandoned their mining claims to head home and join the Confederate forces.

Some of those who remained in the newly proclaimed Colorado Territory formed pro-Confederacy militia groups that became very active in Leadville, Fairplay, and Denver. Mace's Hole, a remote valley east of Pueblo, was a hotbed of Confederate activity. Plans were made by the Rebels to disrupt communications between Union troops at Fort Garland, Fort Lyon, and Camp Weld. Wagon trains carrying military supplies to these forts would be attacked, their goods would be seized, and the flow of federal mail would be interrupted.

There was strong Confederate support in Denver, and the Rebels boldly raised the Confederate flag over a store on Larimer Street in April 1861. Pro-Union forces ripped it down, but conflict increased in Denver, Georgia Gulch, California Gulch, Breckenridge, and other mining camps. Talk of secession intensified during the summer of 1861, and the first governor of the Colorado Territory, William Gilpin, estimated that one out of three Denver residents was a Confederate sympathizer. Southern forces moved into New Mexico and southern Arizona and looked to Colorado's rich gold mines to help finance their war efforts.

Governor Gilpin faced increasing hostilities from the Cheyenne and Arapaho and began recruiting troops of volunteers to defend the territory. Major John Chivington commanded these Colorado volunteer units. The Union army controlled Denver, the territorial capital and the territory's major forts. The southern border of the territory was protected by Fort Garland, which prevented entry from New Mexico by Confederate troops.

The Reynolds brothers, John and Jim, came to the Rockies in the 1859 Pikes Peak Gold Rush. They didn't have any luck prospecting around

Gregory Gulch, so they headed to Tarryall in South Park. Going farther west, they hit paydirt along the South Platte River. These rich placer deposits of gold drew many hopeful prospectors, and Jim Reynolds insisted on "fair play for all," which gave this camp its name, Fairplay. When the Civil War began, the Reynolds brothers abandoned their productive mining claims in Fairplay and joined the Confederates in Mace's Hole.

The Confederate bastion in Mace's Hole was eventually discovered by Union troops from Fort Lyon, who invaded the valley in October 1861. Many Rebels escaped into the surrounding hills, but forty-four were captured, marched to Denver, and thrown into jail. The November 28, 1861 *Colorado City Journal* listed the names of these prisoners, which included Jim and John Reynolds. In February 1862, the Reynolds brothers and thirty-four prisoners escaped with the help of jailer Jackson Robinson, a Southern sympathizer.

In 1864, the Reynolds brothers were enlisted in the Wells Battalion, Third Texas Cavalry, commanded by General Douglas Cooper. They moved into northern New Mexico and southern Colorado with orders to attack Union wagon trains and steal supplies, guns and ammunition. Jim Reynolds led a small group of men into South Park to recruit prospectors and obtain money for the Confederacy by robbing stagecoaches, roadhouses, and travelers. They spent the first night in South Park at Adolphe Guiraud's ranch. The next morning, July 26, they headed for Dan McLaughlin's ranch and stage station eight miles from Fairplay. The stage from Buckskin Joe, which was carrying a gold shipment, always stopped at McLaughlin's to pick up mail and passengers on the way to Denver.

When the stage rolled up that morning, the Confederates moved quickly and grabbed the lead horses. Jim Reynolds, gun drawn, ordered the driver, Abe Williamson, and passenger, Billie McClelland, to get down from the driver's seat with their hands up. They took $400 and a gold watch from McClelland, who was the only passenger and owner of the stage. Then they went through Abe Williamson's pockets and took all he had—$0.16. Abe was furious and loudly protested that robbers usually stole the strong box or cargo—they didn't rob the stage driver.

Reynolds laughed at Williamson as he pried open the strong box, which contained about $1,000 in gold and $3,000 in cash. The robbers opened the U.S. mail bag and rifled through the letters, looking for money. They crammed the loot into their saddlebags and unhitched the team, while Reynolds used an axe to chop the spokes of the stagecoach's wheels. Then they galloped off, taking the horses from the stage, too.

Top: Third Texas Cavalry Regiment flag. *Texas State Library and Archives [306-4049].*

Bottom: A reenactment of a stagecoach holdup. *Huntington Library*.

The Confederates rode several miles north on the road to Denver, stopping briefly at the Michigan House to steal the station's horses and the station master's cash. They rode across South Park's rolling hills, which gradually rose to meet the steep incline of Kenosha Pass. After crossing the pass, they stopped at the Kenosha House, a large stage station that provided meals and lodging for weary travelers. Walking in, they were greeted by the proprietor, but Reynolds responded by waving his revolver in her face and quickly emptying the cash register. He told her that he'd come to Colorado to get money for the Confederate war effort, and he was taking hers.

The gang rode on toward Denver, robbing roadhouses along the way, stealing horses from stage stations, and holding up a wagon or two. News of the robberies spread throughout South Park and the mountain mining camps. Newspapers carried breathless tales of the Confederate robbers, and stage driver Abe Williamson angrily told his story to anyone who'd listen. The Confederates were often described as bloodthirsty bandits and drunken cutthroats who were determined to burn every small settlement, mining camp, or cabin they found. The gang was accused of stealing thousands of dollars, jewelry, and bags of gold dust. Posses were formed to track down the outlaws, who were blamed for every holdup and stage robbery in the Colorado Territory.

Although the outlaws said their loot was going to help fund the Confederacy, many thought they were keeping it for themselves. There are numerous conflicting reports about how long the Reynolds Gang roamed South Park and how many robberies they actually committed. Despite all the lurid newspaper stories, they did not harm anyone or burn anything.

Jack Sparks, a Breckenridge prospector, recruited twelve men from the mining camps in the area to form a posse. Determined to stop the Reynolds Gang, they traveled over the mountains and crossed the Continental Divide, often moving above the timberline at an altitude of around eleven thousand feet. On July 31, they spotted the flickering light of a campfire below in a deep, brushy canyon between Hall Valley and Grant. They dismounted and crept forward through the darkness until they saw several men sitting around a campfire. One of the posse men stepped on a twig, and the sound alerted the gang's lookout. He shouted a warning, and Reynolds and his men dashed for cover in a hail of bullets. They left their supplies, saddles, and extra ammunition behind as they escaped into the nearby trees.

Sparks decided the posse would have better luck tracking these outlaws in the daylight, so they spent the night in the fugitives' camp. The following morning, they found the body of Owen Singletary, a member of the gang who'd been shot during the skirmish. A posse member, Dr. Cooper, cut off his head and put it in a sack. It was preserved in alcohol and displayed in a Fairplay saloon for years.

After they were surprised by the Breckenridge posse, the gang split up and disappeared. Thomas Holliman, Addison Stowe, and John Reynolds vanished into the dense timber of Geneva Gulch and headed south. Holliman could not keep up with them, and before long, Stowe and John Reynolds were several hours ahead of everyone else. At Nineteen Mile Ranch, they stole two horses and helped themselves to supplies and food. Before they left, they drove off the rest of the homesteader's horses so there'd be no fresh mounts if a posse came along.

Hours later, a second group of outlaws, including Jim Reynolds, John Andrews, Thomas Knight, John Bobbitt, and Jackson Robinson, showed up at Nineteen Mile Ranch. They'd been traveling much slower because Reynolds had been shot by the posse and had a severe wound in his arm. They took the rest of the homesteaders' supplies, but all the horses had been driven away earlier by Stowe and John Reynolds.

Meanwhile, another posse of seventy-five angry homesteaders, miners, ranchers, and shopkeepers from Buckskin Joe, Alma, Hamilton, and the surrounding area left Fairplay and headed south to look for the gang. On August 1, they captured Thomas Holliman near the Thirty-One Mile House north of Canon City. Holliman had been walking all night and was exhausted. He was resting in the brush near the road and fell asleep; he was later captured and hauled to the rancher's barn. A committee of prominent citizens questioned him, and when he wouldn't answer them, they decided tougher persuasion was necessary. A noose was looped around Holliman's neck, the rope was tossed over a rafter, and he was hoisted into the air. The committee let him dangle and spin a few minutes and then lowered him to the ground and resumed questioning. When the prisoner's answers weren't satisfactory, the rope was tightened around his neck, and he was strung up again. Holliman, choking and gasping, was raised and lowered until he was half-dead—then he finally told them what he knew. Next, he was put in leg irons, loaded on a horse, and forced to accompany his torturers as they chased down his comrades. Historians believe Holliman told several lies that were mixed with the truth, and some say the posse eventually freed him, and he fled to Oregon.

On August 13, three more fugitives were captured while they were eating breakfast at the ranch of a Southern sympathizer. Then two fugitives were

Looking over the approximate route the Breckenridge posse took while hunting the Reynolds Gang. *Photograph by Tom Williams.*

Stores on Front Street in Fairplay, circa 1888. *Park County Local History Archive.*

found asleep, rolled up in their blankets. They were rudely awakened around 3:00 a.m. and taken into custody. The five prisoners were separated and interrogated, and they maintained they were Confederates acting on military orders of General Cooper. They were taken to Denver by U.S. Marshal Hunt, jailed on August 20, and held for trial. Holliman's whereabouts were unknown. The information the committee had obtained by torturing him was termed "testimony" and published in the August 31 and September 1, 1864 issues of the *Daily Mining Journal.*

John Reynolds and Addison Stowe followed the Arkansas River south of Canon City to the Jerome Ranch, where they built a crude raft. Despite high water and rough rapids, they managed to cross the river. They continued through southern Colorado, where many people supported the Confederacy and helped them. They kept a southwesterly course, crossed the Cucharas River, skirted the Sangre de Cristo Mountains, passed the Spanish Peaks, and disappeared.

In Denver, Major Chivington, commander of the Colorado Militia, insisted that Marshal Hunt turn Jim Reynolds and his four comrades over to him. At first, Hunt refused, but Chivington, an intimidating bully, seized the men in a show of military force and announced that he was going to try them by military commission. He sent a telegram to his commander, General Curtis in Kansas, to announce that he had "five notorious guerillas in custody" and that they would be tried by military commission. He asked, "If convicted can I shoot them?" Without waiting for an answer, Chivington secretly put the prisoners on trial for murder, rape, and robbery. Eyewitness testimony proved that the men in the gang had never raped or killed anyone—they'd only robbed stagecoaches and Union supply trains. They were found guilty of robbery, a crime punishable by a prison term. There are some reports that they were given death sentences, which was too severe a punishment for the crime of robbery.

General Curtis's answer came quickly. He said that Chivington did not have the authority to try anyone, and he could not shoot the prisoners. He ordered Chivington to escort the five prisoners to Fort Lyon. From there, they were to be transferred to Fort Leavenworth, where they could be tried and sentenced by General Curtis. Chivington did not tell his commander that he had already unlawfully tried the prisoners and sentenced them to death.

Around September 1, Chivington ordered Captain Theodore Cree and one hundred men of the Third Colorado Cavalry to take the prisoners to Fort Lyon. About thirty-two miles south of Denver, they reached Russellville, an abandoned townsite. Cree left a small detail of soldiers, commanded by Sergeant Allen Shaw, there with the prisoners, while the main body continued to Fort Lyon. The shackled prisoners were tied to trees, and Sergeant Shaw ordered his men to execute them. Every soldier refused, protesting that these men were military prisoners, guilty only of robbery. Once again, Sergeant Shaw ordered his men to fire at the prisoners. This time, all but one trooper raised their rifles and shot over the heads of the prisoners. One man, Jim Reynolds, slumped over dead, killed by Abe Williamson, the stage driver who held a grudge because they had robbed him. He was a member of the Colorado Cavalry and had volunteered for this task. Furiously yelling at the troopers, Sergeant Shaw raised his rifle and shot a prisoner in the chest. The man collapsed. Revolted by what he'd done, Shaw turned away, saying he just couldn't kill the rest of the prisoners. Then Abe Williamson, screaming and cursing his fellow soldiers, raised his rifle and shot the rest of the prisoners.

The execution party, sickened by this brutal experience, climbed on their horses and rode away, leaving the bodies unburied. These murders were ordered by Colonel Chivington, who threatened to "hang any SOB who buried their bodies and did not leave them to rot on the prairie." The soldiers were ordered to report that the prisoners were shot while trying to escape. Captain Cree questioned each man in Shaw's unit individually to see if he had his "facts straight." Every one of them parroted the official story of the "escape attempt."

There were immediate questions about the bloody end of the Reynolds Gang. Uncle Dick Wooten demanded to know how five men could escape when they were shackled and tied to trees. There was growing outrage and calls for an investigation. In 1865, U.S. Attorney General Browne filed an official protest with General Curtis: "If they were Confederate soldiers carrying out orders as they claimed, they should have been held to determine their status and then tried." He concluded, "On behalf of our people I demand that these outrages be investigated."

The fury over the killings at Russellville in September 1864 was lost in the aftermath of Chivington's actions two months later, in November. Colonel Chivington ordered six hundred soldiers of the Third Colorado Cavalry to attack a sleeping camp of peaceful Cheyenne and Arapaho at Sand Creek before dawn on November 29, 1864. Hundreds of women, children, and elders were killed, and their bodies were mutilated. The Sand Creek Massacre is one of the worst atrocities ever committed by U.S. soldiers. It was investigated in 1865 by the War Department and two special congressional committees. Chivington's actions were condemned, and he was removed as commander of the Military District of Colorado. John Evans was forced to resign as governor of the Colorado Territory.

Officials who investigated the massacre at Sand Creek took a closer look at Chivington's part in the Russellville killings. The men in Sergeant Shaw's execution squad testified about what really happened that day. Captain Cree confessed that the prisoners had been killed and their bodies left unburied on Chivington's orders. Judge Advocate General Holt reviewed the records of the secret Reynolds trial and overturned the convictions and death sentences. He posthumously pardoned the five men on February 6, 1865. Under post–Civil War amnesty, criminal charges could not be filed against Chivington.

Author's note: Prisoner John Andrews survived being shot in the chest and managed to escape his bonds and crawl to an abandoned cabin nearby. It's rumored he was helped by a friend, and after his wound healed, he went to Taos. Both he and Stowe were killed while stealing horses in New Mexico.

John Reynolds hid out in Santa Fe using the assumed name Will Wallace. Eventually, he returned to the holdup business with another outlaw, Albert Brown. In 1871, Reynolds was shot while stealing horses and suffered a mortal wound. Realizing his time was running out, he told Brown about the 1864 robberies. He said,

> *Jim and me buried the treasure the morning before the posse attack on Geneva Gulch. You go up above there a little ways and find where one of our horses mired down in a swamp. Up at the head of the gulch, we turned to the right and followed the mountain around a little farther, and just above the head of Deer Creek, we found an old prospect hole at about timberline. There we placed $40,000 in greenbacks, wrapped in silk oilcloth and three cans of gold dust. We filled the mouth of the hole up with stones and ten steps below, struck a butcher knife into a tree about four feet from the ground and broke the handle off and left it pointing toward the mouth of the hole.*

He drew a map of where he and his brother hid the loot. John Reynolds died in October 1871. He was about thirty-one years old.

Around 1873, Albert Brown was arrested in a robbery attempt in Denver and jailed by City Marshal Dave Cook. He learned Brown's story, obtained a copy of the treasure map, and included it in the second edition of his book, *Hands Up! or Thirty-Five Years of Detective Work in the Mountains and on the Plains.* Brown escaped from the Denver Jail and fled to Laramie, Wyoming Territory, where he was killed in a drunken brawl.

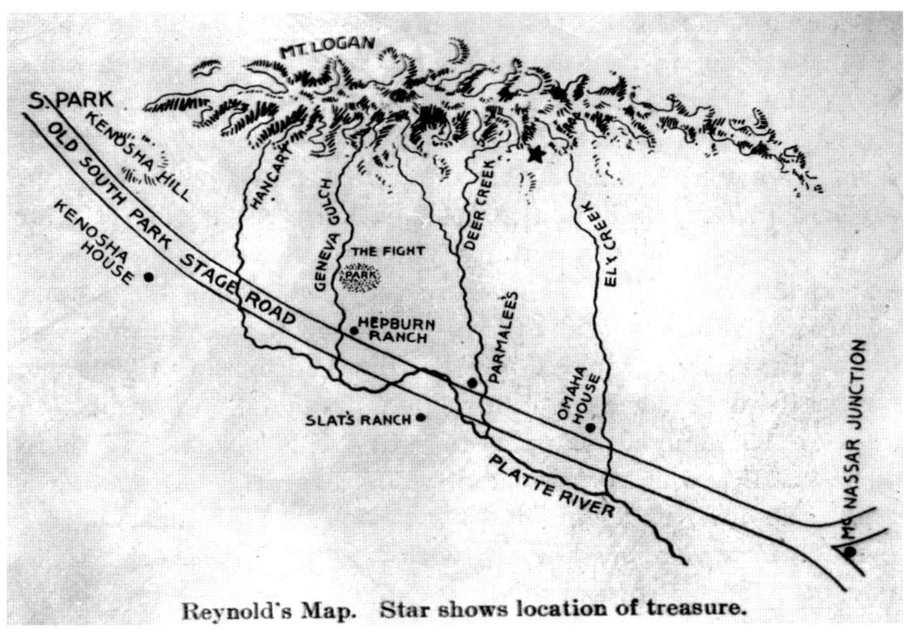

Reynolds Gang treasure map. *Illustration from* Hands Up, *by David J. Cook.*

Albert Brown and a partner made three unsuccessful attempts to find the Reynolds treasure, but the area's landmarks had been obliterated by landslides and a forest fire. Over the years, treasure hunters have looked for the Reynolds loot, but no one has found it.

6

DOC SHORES ALWAYS GETS HIS MAN

"You're the damndest bloodhound I've ever seen!" exclaimed a fugitive to Doc Shores. The sheriff had traveled over six thousand miles on foot and horseback and by train across Colorado, Kansas, and Utah to track down and capture these train robbers. The lawman, respected for his detective abilities and tracking skills, had a reputation for his fairness, iron will, and grim determination to "get his man."

Doc was elected sheriff of Gunnison County, Colorado, in 1883 and took over in January 1884. There was plenty of crime and a woeful lack of law and order in Gunnison when Doc arrived in 1880. Most criminals weren't caught, and the ones who were either escaped or never went to trial. Doc was disgusted and decided to run for sheriff in 1883, easily defeating the incumbent. He became Gunnison County's third sheriff, and within a couple of years, he'd run down several horse thieves, put a ring of rustlers behind bars, solved a murder, and single-handedly held off a mob that was determined to lynch his prisoner. He was appointed a deputy U.S. marshal, which gave him the authority to pursue criminals across county and state lines.

When he took over as sheriff, Cyrus "Doc" Shores was already well versed in the ways of the frontier West. He was named "Doc" after the doctor who delivered him, and as a boy, he hated sitting in a classroom. His uncle taught him to identify animal tracks and how to set a steel trap when he was seven years old. Doc usually carried an old flintlock to school and often played hooky to go hunting in the Michigan woods.

In 1866, when he was twenty-two, Doc headed for the Montana Territory, where he worked on a Missouri River steamship keeping the crew's dinner table supplied with fresh game. He saved his wages, bought a freight wagon and team of oxen and hauled supplies to Montana gold mining camps. In the Wyoming Territory, he delivered railroad ties to the Union Pacific, which was laying tracks for the first transcontinental railroad. During the Plains Wars in the 1870s, he hauled freight and military supplies to army posts in Colorado and northern New Mexico and fought off hostile attacks several times. Realizing the profits he could gain selling beef to eastern markets, Doc decided to go into the cattle business.

Doc Shores, the fearless Colorado lawman. *Wild West History Association.*

Doc drove cattle up the Chisholm Trail to Kansas shipping depots for seven years, enduring blizzards, tornados, dangerous river crossings and quicksand, lightning, massive thunderstorms, and stampedes. He was married in 1877, and in 1880, he sold his cattle and headed for the booming town of Gunnison, Colorado. Doc and his wife, Agnes, arrived in Colorado in May 1880, bought two freight wagons and soon had a thriving business hauling freight to the silver mining camps in the nearby mountains.

Gunnison was a supply center for the mines and surrounding cattle ranches. A school was built, and the town's fledgling newspaper reported the arrival of the Sanderson Stage Line. When the Denver and Rio Grande steamed into Gunnison in August 1881, it was greeted with cheers and celebrations. The Denver and South Park Railroad was laying its tracks west and arrived in September 1882. The railroads played an essential role in the development of Colorado, and they slowly replaced stage lines in the 1880s. These trains carried currency, payrolls, financial instruments and gold, silver, and other precious metals. They soon became the slow-moving targets of criminals.

The Denver and Rio Grande Railroad, the first railroad in Colorado, began operating in 1870 and was never robbed—until November 3, 1887. In the early morning hours of November 3, the Denver and Rio Grande train steamed out of the Grand Junction Station, headed south

D&RGW locomotive, photographed at Cimarron, Colorado. A locomotive like this one was robbed at the Unaweep Switch in 1887. *Colorado Railroad Museum.*

toward Delta. About five miles southeast of town, the tracks ran between the Gunnison River and a high cliff at Unaweep Switch. When the train rounded a sharp curve, its headlights lit up a large pile of rocks and timbers that was blocking the tracks. The engineer quickly pulled on the brakes and stopped the train. Four masked men suddenly appeared with their guns drawn. One climbed into the cab and ordered the engineer and fireman to get out. He held them at gunpoint while three others hurried to the mail car and banged loudly on the door.

The agent inside was asleep, and when he woke up, he thought they were in Delta, so he opened the door. He was confronted by three masked men with their guns drawn, and they quickly climbed into the mail car. They rifled through the mail bags but found little of value, so they jumped out and moved on to the express and baggage cars. Their shouts of "Open up!" were ignored, and the agent refused to unlock the door until the angry outlaws threatened to blow up the train.

There were two safes in this car: a small one that contained about $150 and a larger one that held several thousand dollars. The agent opened the small safe but, despite the gun pressed against his head, swore he didn't have the combination for the large safe. He said only certain officials along the train's route had that combination. The gang leader became angry as the agent frantically twirled the safe's dial, all while insisting he didn't know the combination. Finally, the robbers were convinced, took the $150, decided not to rob the passengers, and quickly disappeared into the night.

The barricade was removed, and the train continued to Delta, where the sheriff was notified. A posse was organized in Grand Junction, and its members spent two days searching the holdup area for clues. They found nothing and returned empty-handed to town.

Doc Shores received a telegram from the U.S. marshal in Denver asking him to join the search for the train robbers. Railroad executives added their pleas, and the Denver and Rio Grande Express Company offered a $3,000 reward. This total was increased by another $1,000 from the federal government. In those days, lawmen were allowed to collect rewards that were offered for the arrest of criminals, and the money was a helpful supplement to their low salaries.

As a U.S. marshal, Doc had the authority to pursue the train robbers across state and county lines. He learned from the train engineer that the robbers had remained calm and cool, although they seemed to be new at robbing trains. They forgot to check the pockets of the train men, one of whom had $119 in his wallet. Doc said the large safe was rumored to contain as much as $75,000, but the robbers' total take "did not exceed $150."

Doc recruited his brother-in-law, M.L. Allison, who was on vacation visiting in Gunnison. They caught the train from Gunnison to Grand Junction and headed for Unaweep Switch. Arriving with the first light of dawn on November 5, they looked for signs of the robbers. Doc was well known for his tracking skills and methodically searched one side of the Gunnison River and then crossed and searched the opposite bank. The men spent two days searching and then caught the train back to Grand Junction, where they spent the night in a hotel. They were on the job by dawn the next morning and finally found the footprints of two men in the mud headed toward rugged Bangs Canyon. Doc was puzzled because there were no hoofprints.

Doc Shores's wilderness tracking skills were invaluable as the men followed the robbers' footprints into Bangs Canyon. They rode their horses down the steep, brushy slopes until the animals began slipping and falling. The ground became so rocky that they were forced to leave their horses behind and go on foot. Doc kept a sharp eye out for tiny signs that the robbers had passed here: scratches from boot heels on the surface of the rocks, scuffs in the dirt, scattered leaves and broken twigs. Doc and Allison followed the canyon for miles but turned back when the sun went down. Hours later, they finally returned to Grand Junction, exhausted and cold, and collapsed on their hotel beds.

The following morning, Doc and Allison were back in Bangs Canyon riding rented horses. They rode, walked, and stumbled over loose rocks, and climbed around huge boulders, working their way twenty miles down the canyon. Doc lost his footing and fell about fifteen feet from a precipice and landed in a water hole. Luckily, he wasn't seriously injured and carried on, bruised and soaking wet. The men found a plug of tobacco and a small pocketknife, positive signs that they were on the thieves' trail. They reached the Gunnison River when it was quite dark and decided to turn back. The return climb back up the canyon on foot was difficult because it was pitch dark, and they had trouble finding their horses. They finally returned to their hotel about an hour before dawn.

The following day, Doc shipped in his own horses from Gunnison, and he and Allison were joined by Jim Duckworth, a railroad detective. They headed down Unaweep Canyon, which runs parallel to Bangs Canyon, and went farther south. They spent the night at a cow camp near the present town of Gateway. Doc engaged a cowboy to guide them as they followed the Dolores River through wild country toward Sinbad Valley. They made their way carefully down precipitous slopes that were so steep they had to lead their horses, but the animals still slipped and fell several times.

They were caught in a miserable, soaking rain and spent the night outdoors in the cold, huddled under a single blanket, The next morning, the rain turned to snow, and a blizzard blew in, but luckily, they found an abandoned moonshiner's dugout. The wind howled, and the snow piled up, so they spent three days in the dugout, which was well-stocked with food and moonshine.

They moved on when the weather cleared, but Duckworth had become ill and had a difficult time staying in the saddle. A cowboy named Denning guided them into Paradox Valley, but there wasn't a trace of the four robbers, so they turned around. They couldn't go back the way they'd come because the canyon was blocked by twelve feet of snow. They worked their way south and waited out the storm at a ranch near Uravan. They turned east and, after a difficult journey up the San Miguel River, reached Placerville. Doc and Duckworth took the stage to the depot at Dallas, where the ill detective boarded the train for Grand Junction and medical attention.

Doc, Denning, and Allison went north to Delta, where they learned that four men had built a boat on the Gunnison River near town. They talked to people who'd seen the four and knew the names of two of the men, who were brothers from Kansas. When the boat was completed, the four men loaded their supplies and guns, climbed in, and headed upriver one day before the train robbery.

Shores and his party returned to Grand Junction and searched along the river for the boat. They swam their horses along each side of the river and found it hidden in brush several miles downriver. Doc made a quick trip to Denver to update D&RG officials and the Pinkerton Detective Agency. He told them the robbers had been identified as Ed Rhodes, Bob Boyd (or Boyle), and brothers Bob and Jack Smith.

The manager of the railroad's express company received a tip and insisted Shores investigate. This turned out to be a wild goose chase, and Shores, Allison, and Denning spent several days and nights in another winter storm. They all got sick, and Denning was hospitalized after he became critically ill with pneumonia. Doc received the sad news that his detective friend Jim Duckworth had died from pneumonia.

Allison recuperated and returned home, and Denning slowly recovered. Doc was surprised to find the boat was gone from its hiding place. Tracks indicated the robbers had come back, climbed in the boat, and headed west on the Grand (Colorado) River. Doc rode downriver sixty miles to Cisco, Utah, and on to Green River, where he learned that four men, who had arrived in a boat, caught a train north to Price. At this inopportune moment, Shores was summoned back to Denver by the D&RG branch manager, who'd heard a rumor that the robbers from Kansas had returned home. Doc asked Allison and his undersheriff to head for Utah while the robbers' trail was hot. The Mesa County sheriff joined them, and they left for Price.

Meanwhile, Shores and Pinkerton Agent Charlie Siringo caught the train to Kansas, 385 miles away. They quickly determined that this was another wild goose chase, so they jumped on a train back to Denver, which was another 385 miles of travel.

Meanwhile, Allison's group had tracked down and arrested the Smith brothers and Ed Rhodes in Utah and were returning on the train to Colorado. Doc caught the first train headed west and was able to intercept the eastbound train carrying Allison and his group. He greeted the handcuffed prisoners, "You fellas have sure been causin' me a lot of grief, trackin' you all over the country!" Ed Rhodes replied wryly, "You're the damndest bloodhound I ever seen!" Despite their situation, the outlaws were in a jovial mood and spent the rest of the journey joking and comparing notes with the lawmen. Rhodes said he was actually glad they'd been caught: "We've been livin' outdoors in this weather, freezin' and starvin' like wild animals." Jack Smith agreed, "I ain't been warm or had a square meal since the robbery."

Doc took the three robbers to jail in Denver, where they faced federal charges. He trailed Bob Wallace, the fourth outlaw, to Kansas and back to Utah, where Doc arrested him. The four train robbers were tried and sentenced to time in federal prison. Shores had traveled six hundred miles on foot and horseback and around six thousand miles by train, crossing Colorado, Kansas, and Utah in pursuit of the train robbers. He was pleased to collect the $4,000 reward.

Doc Shores met Tom Horn for the first time in 1890 while pursuing a thief who'd stolen several horses and fled to Arizona. Working together, they captured the outlaw and retrieved the stolen animals. Shores recommended Horn to the Pinkerton Detective Agency, who hired him. Horn spent several years as a Pinkerton agent and worked with Doc Shores pursuing the Cotopaxi train robbers in 1891.

On the evening of August 31, 1891, the Denver & Rio Grande was flagged down at a remote spot where the Arkansas River Canyon narrows near the tiny settlement of Cotopaxi. Masked men forced the flagman to wave his lantern at the oncoming train. The engineer saw him and applied the brakes, and the huge wheels of the locomotive ground to a stop. Several masked men stepped out of the brush, their guns drawn. One climbed into the cab and ordered the engineer and fireman to get out and join the flagman by the tracks. The masked man kept his gun trained on them as two other masked men ran to the mail car and started shooting at the door. The agent inside yelled and slid the door open. The robbers scrambled inside but realized they'd made a mistake when they saw the mail sacks. One robber grabbed the agent's gold watch that was lying on a shelf as they jumped out and headed for the express car. The threat of dynamite opened the door, revealing two safes inside. At gunpoint, the agent opened the small safe, which yielded about $600 in gold and $3,000 in cash. The robbers seemed to know the agent wouldn't have the combination for the large safe, so they grabbed their loot and jumped from the express car. They scrambled down the steep slope toward the river and disappeared into the night. A few minutes later, there was a pounding of hooves as the robbers galloped off. Most of the passengers remained asleep during the robbery, and those who knew something was happening stayed quietly in their rail car.

Within twenty-four hours of the robbery, H.G. Kramer, the general manager of the railroad, had persuaded Doc to join the investigation, headquartered at Texas Creek, seven miles east of Cotopaxi. Doc and Kramer took the train to Texas Creek, which looked like a Wild West boom town, overflowing with sheriffs, cowboys, posses, and special investigators.

The flagman and engineer described the robbers, who were led by a powerfully built man with a peg leg. They said his slender right-hand man stood out because he was wearing a black derby hat, and noted that the two outlaws guarding the railroad men looked much younger than the others. Shores, Kramer, several local deputies, and Tom Horn of the Pinkerton Detective Agency headed to the holdup site at Cotopaxi. Doc observed that the robbery had taken place directly across the river from the ranch house of Dick McCoy, a notorious horse thief and rustler. "Old Dick's" place was a known hideout for the Dalton Gang and other outlaws.

When Doc, Kramer, Horn, and several deputies rode up to McCoy's place, Old Dick came out. "You're just in time for dinner, sheriff," he said, inviting them in. The atmosphere around the table became tense when Doc casually asked McCoy's teenage son questions about the robbery. Old Dick advised his son to "get to eatin'," and there was no more talk about the train robbery. After dinner, Doc and the others crossed the river to the holdup site, but any clues had been trampled and obliterated by the careless posses inspecting the area. Doc expanded his search and found footprints, a pipe, cigarette butts, and burnt matches where the robbers had waited for the train. On his hands and knees, Doc studied the footprints and identified circular indentations that could have been made by someone with a peg leg.

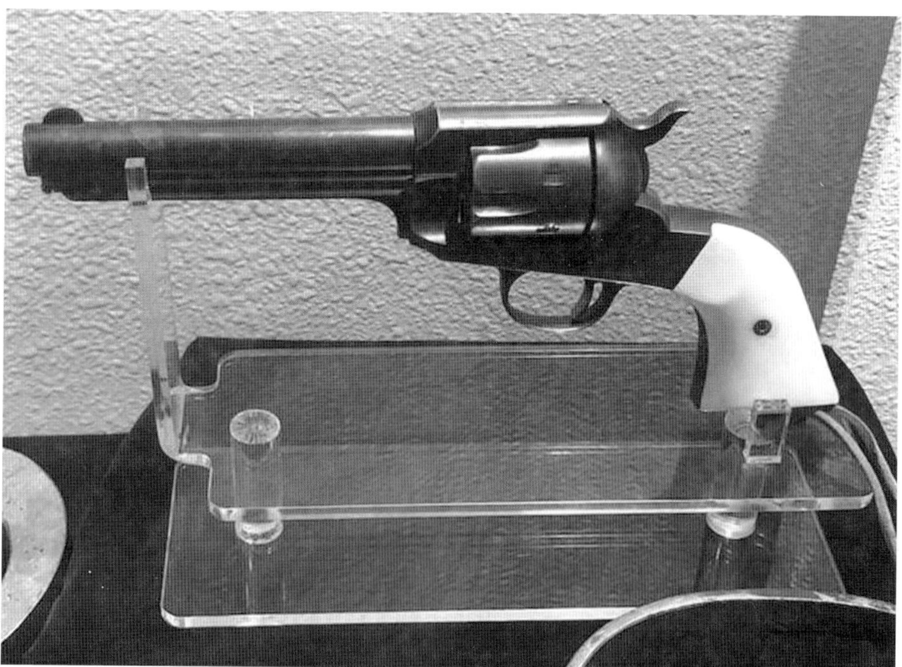

Doc Shores's pearl-handled revolver. *Museum of Western Colorado.*

Later while chatting with a Cotopaxi storekeeper, Doc learned that Burt Curtis and Peg Leg Watson had recently been released from prison, and he decided they might be the holdup men. Curtis always wore a derby hat, and Watson had lost his leg in the Civil War. Shores found the outlaws' trail, which led away from the robbery site, and he, Tom Horn, and a deputy followed it into the rugged Sangre de Cristo Mountains. They made camp at timberline, an altitude around eleven thousand feet, and were miserably cold. They rolled up in their bedrolls with their feet near the fire, but they were so chilled that no one slept well. Doc later said that they nearly burned the soles off their boots trying to keep warm. In the morning, they hurriedly crossed the crest of the mountains and descended into the San Luis Valley.

They picked up the trail of four horsemen and followed it into New Mexico and then back into Colorado, where they finally caught up with the four. They were severely disappointed when they discovered they'd spent days trailing cowboys who were looking for stray cattle. They returned to Cotopaxi and learned that another posse had been following them! This widespread confusion was due to the large number of posses, lawmen, railroad agents, and detectives who were in the field looking for the outlaws.

Horn and Shores learned that a man wearing a derby hat and another with a peg leg had passed through Trinidad, traveling east. They loaded their Winchesters, saddles, and supplies for a long chase and headed into eastern New Mexico, where they picked up the robbers' trail. They spent long hours in the saddle, starting before dawn and riding until after dark. They covered thirty to forty miles a day and maintained this grueling pace for forty-three days. They crossed into the Texas Panhandle and followed the Washita River into the Indian Territory of Oklahoma. The outlaws didn't know they were being followed, so they didn't avoid small towns and settlements. When the outlaws stopped for the occasional drink, they often bragged that they were wanted men and would kill anyone foolish enough to follow them.

South of Anadarko, Oklahoma Territory, a teenager told the lawmen that two men who fit the outlaws' description were staying at a local ranch. Before dawn the following morning, Doc and Horn, guided by a deputy marshal, stealthily approached the ranch on foot. They surprised Curtis and took him into custody, and they learned that Peg Leg Watson was gone but was expected to return in a few days. Since there was no jail or place to hold Curtis, they decided Doc would start back to Denver with him, while Horn and the deputy marshal waited for Watson. Since they didn't have shackles, Doc improvised some from a rusty farm chain and an old padlock. There was no key, so Doc used a nail to open the padlock. He shackled his prisoner, loaded him onto a horse, and they rode to Gainseville, Texas, where the sheriff met them with a set of sturdy shackles.

With the prisoner secured, Doc boarded the train and locked one of his prisoner's shackles to the leg of his passenger seat. He had to stay alert and keep his eyes on Curtis, who was waiting for his chance to escape. When they reached Clayton, New Mexico, Doc was relieved when two Pinkerton agents boarded the train to escort them the rest of the way to Denver. The police met them at Denver's Union Station and took Curtis to jail. A day or two later, Horn arrived on the train with Peg Leg Watson handcuffed to his wrist. When their case was tried, both robbers were found guilty and sentenced to life in prison.

Peg Leg Watson served twenty years and died in prison. Curtis served twenty years before Doc helped him get his life sentence commuted. After Curtis was released, Doc received a letter from him inviting him to meet in the Wet Mountains. Curtis said they could dig up and share the money and gold that he and Watson had buried after the Cotopaxi train robbery. Shores replied that, in good conscience, he must decline the offer. This was the only time in all of Doc Shores's years as a lawman that a train robber offered to share his loot.

On December 11, 1891, Doc received a telegram from William Grant, the superintendent of the Colorado Coal and Iron Company in Crested Butte, a coal mining town. The telegram said, "Fans have been stopped by striking coal miners. Mines rapidly filling with gas. Explosion imminent which will blow up much of the town as well as the mine. Your help needed immediately to protect life and property." Doc knew quick action was needed, because built-up methane gas in a mine will quickly explode—but fans can remove it. Crested Butte had suffered a disaster in 1884, when methane gas exploded in the Jokerville Mine, killing fifty-nine miners.

Doc got a handful of warrants for the strike leaders and recruited twenty-five deputies, including his best gunmen, and then climbed on a train provided by the railroad. As the train neared Crested Butte around midnight, the engineer turned off the headlight, didn't blow the whistle, and pushed the sheriff's well-lit rail car toward the mine entrance. A crowd of miners suddenly rushed out of the darkness, shooting at them. Doc and his men hustled out of the car in a hail of bullets and dashed to shelter at the mine entrance. They crouched down, ready to return the gunfire, as Doc instructed everyone to aim at the miners' legs—he hoped to avoid killing anyone. Doc's men opened fire, and about thirty miners fell as the rest beat a hasty retreat. Doc and his deputies dashed up the stairs nearby to an elevated, covered platform that overlooked the mine and the town.

The following day dragged on with no more gunfire. The doctor was busy patching up the thirty-six miners who'd been shot (only one was seriously wounded). Since Doc and his deputies couldn't go into Crested Butte, they spent a very cold night on the elevated platform without food, fire, or blankets. The following day, a small delegation of miners gathered beneath the elevated platform and demanded the posse leave town. When Doc told them to turn on the fans to dispel the dangerous gas in the mine, the miners refused and left.

Doc's men were dreading another cold night on the platform when they heard bells jingling and saw a sleigh headed their way. It stopped below the platform, and the driver shouted that the sleigh was from the people of Gunnison who heard they needed some help. The sleigh was piled high with warm blankets, food, and medical supplies. The driver said that a special train carrying thirty-five volunteers and a doctor was on the way to Crested Butte. He added that Gunnison folks were worried that Doc and his deputies would be "all shot up." The sheriff later wrote in his memoir that it was good to learn that he and his deputies had not been forgotten. He said this was "one of the most heart-warming experiences" of his life.

The gas, meanwhile, had been building up in the mine, increasing fears of an explosion. Doc threatened to move his men and said they would no longer protect the entrance unless there was action. The mine superintendent finally got the fans started, clearing out the dangerous gas and reducing the tension. The labor commissioner arrived the next day with the train that was carrying Gunnison volunteers. He met with about two hundred striking miners, most of whom were Italian or Austrian and spoke little English. Another meeting was set up between representatives of the strikers and mine officials for the following morning.

Doc and his four top gunfighters, wearing a six-shooter on each hip, stood by as the two groups tried to resolve their issues in a stormy all-day session. Doc was satisfied because no shots had been fired, and some progress had been made. There were several more meetings between the opposing factions, and compromises were made. Doc decided he could safely serve the warrants and arrest the strike instigators and troublemakers. He and his most experienced deputies and well-known gunfighters first went to the train depot, where striking miners met the train daily to intercept strikebreakers. Shores recognized one of the troublemakers, and he was taken into custody. A crowd watched, but there was no trouble.

Next, Doc and his men walked into town to serve the remaining warrants and make arrests. The *Rocky Mountain News* of December 19, 1891, reported, "Shores arrived with such well known men as the Marlow boys of Telluride [*sic*], Colorado, who are wanted in Texas, but whom Governor Routt refused to extradite. John Watson of western Colorado who has the reputation of having killed several men…and several other well-known gentlemen who are very handy with firearms in such a situation." Doc Shores recalled the tense moments:

> *We walked two abreast, each of us carrying a Winchester rifle….My deputies and I held our rifles in both hands as we entered town, prepared for any emergency….By this time, nearly a thousand people lined the street watching our progress with interest. When we came to John Follette's saloon, I went inside carrying my rifle in one hand and a warrant in the other. Follette was a prominent man about town, and the spectators for the first time began showing excitement. As they closed in around the posse to better see the show, Jack Watson and the Marlow boys raised their guns and ordered the onlookers back.*

Doc arrested Follette with no trouble, although his wife was very upset and created "quite an emotional scene." Two other strikers were arrested, and Doc took them to Gunnison and jailed them while the deputies returned to guard the mine.

The following morning was pay day, and as the troublemakers came to collect their checks, they were arrested. By the end of the day, Doc remarked, "Before long, I had made quite a haul." He and several deputies took the prisoners back to Gunnison on a special train that stopped near the LaVeta Hotel, the town's most elegant showplace. A judge met them and bound the prisoners over to district court for attempting to kill Doc and his deputies. They were held in the Gunnison Jail to await trial.

Doc served eight years as the sheriff of Gunnison County and did not run for a third term. When the strikers came up for trial in 1892, Doc and the district attorney decided not to prosecute them, so they were released from jail. Doc accepted a position as a special investigator for the Denver and Rio Grande Express Company and spent the next twenty-four years in this job. Doc was respected for his fairness, courage, and determination in tracking down lawbreakers, earning him the nickname, the "Bloodhound."

When he was in his eighties, Doc wrote about his life on the frontier and his experiences as a lawman in his memoirs. Wilson Rockwell edited the

Elk Avenue, Crested Butte. *Crested Butte Museum.*

La Veta Hotel, Gunnison. *W. Jackson, 1882–1900; Denver Public Library Special Collections [WHJ-856].*

manuscripts, concentrating on Doc's eight years as the sheriff of Gunnison County, for *Memoirs of a Lawman*. Doc Shores's complete memoir of unedited manuscripts is now held by the Western History Department of the Denver Public Library. Cyrus "Doc" Shores died on October 12, 1934, one month short of his ninetieth birthday. People cane from miles around to honor Doc's memory when he was buried in the Gunnison Cemetery.

7

JIM CLARK

LAWMAN AND OUTLAW

Jim Clark was a lawman who occasionally stepped over the line into the outlaw world. His good friend Doc Shores, the sheriff of Gunnison County and a U.S. marshal, knew that Jim insisted on law and order inside Telluride's city limits, but he broke that law every once in a while outside of town.

Once, Clark unbuttoned his shirt and pulled out a fat roll of bills from a secret pocket and confided to Shores, "This was my cut of the Telluride bank robbery." He was referring to the June 24, 1889 robbery of the San Miguel Valley Bank that launched Butch Cassidy's outlaw career. Clark had arranged to be out of town the day of the holdup, and his outlaw friends left his share of the loot, $2,200, hidden under a log by the trail.

Shores was pleased that Clark had taken him into his confidence but said that he was "surprised that Jim was an accomplice of the bank robbers." There were rumors that Clark had plenty of outlaw contacts outside the city limits. When the mines sent freight wagons loaded with large shipments of gold and silver to the railroad depot at Dallas for shipment to Denver, there were sometimes mysterious tips to outlaws. When the freight wagons were held up, there were more whispers that Jim Clark had received a cut of the take. Shores wrote, "While it was generally believed he was involved in stage holdups outside of Telluride, he was given credit for keeping all kinds of lawlessness outside the city limits." Doc said that Clark gave him many valuable leads about crimes in which he or his friends didn't participate.

Above: The Mahr building was once the San Miguel Valley Bank, the site of Butch Cassidy's first bank robbery in 1889. *C. Highsmith, Library of Congress, https://www.loc.gov/item/2017686325/.*

Opposite: Mahr building historical plaque. *Photograph by Tom Williams.*

One evening, when Shores was visiting, Clark pried up one of his cabin's floorboards and brought out his "business suit": a long, dark overcoat, slouch hat, and a set of false black whiskers. When Clark wore this disguise, the scraggly whiskers and old hat hid his face and made him hard to recognize, especially in the dark. Clark said he put on his disguise and hid along the trail to town and robbed miners of their gold. He justified this saying, "They'd just throw the gold away in a saloon or sporting house. I can put that money to much better use."

Shores continued in his memoir,

> *It might be wondered why I chose to maintain a friendship with a man of such strange contrasts. In spite of certain criminal tendencies which shocked me, I liked and admired him in many ways. He was a man of strong character, great courage, and a fanatical loyalty to his friends. He had his own set of standards which he lived up to—so he was not without principle. He was a capable peace officer and probably did more than any other to bring law and order to Telluride.*

Researchers looking into the life story of Jim Clark encounter many contradictions, starting with his name. Some historians say he was born "Clark," while others are certain his name was "Cummings." Jim's father died when he was a baby, and his mother later married a man whose surname is still in question. In his autobiography, *Memoirs of a Lawman*, Doc Shores said that his friend was born in 1841 in Missouri and that "his real name was Jim Cummings." Shores added, "His mother's second marriage was to a man named Clark."

Jim committed his first criminal act at seventeen, when he stole a mule from his stepfather and rode off to San Antonio with a friend. The boys sold the mule and spent the money on clothes, high-top boots with "stars on the front," and a pair of six-shooters. They used the guns to hold up a rancher outside of San Antonio and relieve him of $1,400. When Jim returned home, his stepfather was furious about the theft of his mule and refused to have anything more to do with him. Jim's mother welcomed him back and even hid the stolen money so his stepfather wouldn't learn about this second, more serious crime.

According to some accounts, Jim became acquainted with William Quantrill, a schoolteacher who boarded at the Clark home. By the time the Civil War broke out, Jim was a twenty-year-old, tall, burly, broad-shouldered young man. A crack shot and skilled rider, Jim was one of the first to join Quantrill's band of guerrillas. which included the James brothers and the Youngers. Some historians suggest he was "Jim Cummings," Quantrill's favored lieutenant. Occasionally, he reminisced and told stories about those wild days. Once, while riding alone on a road in southern Missouri, Jim said he came upon four Union cavalrymen who were looking for members of Quantrill's guerrilla gang. Clark didn't waste time talking; he just took the reins with his teeth, grabbed both his revolvers, spurred his horse, and charged the soldiers at top speed, shooting and yelling like a madman. When the dust cleared, there were four dead Yankees.

In his later years, Jim made no secret of his Southern sympathies and claimed he'd completed several secret missions for Quantrill. Newspaper journalists speculated that after Quantrill was killed, and the war ended, many of his followers, including Clark, rode with outlaw gangs, holding up stages and robbing banks.

Clark drifted into Leadville, a booming mining camp whose rich silver deposits drew in thousands of prospectors, businessmen, gamblers, "soiled doves," dance hall girls, and charlatans. He worked in the mines and was in top physical shape when the world heavyweight champion came to town. The champ promised $100 to any man who could climb into the ring, box with him for five minutes, and remain standing. Clark, who was as large as the champion, accepted the challenge and got into the ring as his supporters cheered and clapped. Jim slugged it out with the champ and managed to stay on his feet to win the money, but he took quite a beating. He wasn't a trained boxer, and he often said that the $100 was the hardest money he ever earned.

An illustration of Telluride Marshal Jim Clark. *From the* Rocky Mountain News, *circa 1895.*

In 1887, Jim Clark rode into Telluride, where he was hired by a crew that was digging a pipeline into town. Swinging a pickaxe was hard work, but Jim stuck to it. He noticed that a gang of rowdy troublemakers was creating chaos, always getting drunk and shooting up the place. They busted up saloons and gambling halls, put bullet holes in store windows, and sent everyone scrambling for cover. The townspeople were terrorized, and the city marshal was afraid of them and did nothing.

Jim quickly sized up the situation and made a plan. One day, when the gang was on another rampage and the marshal went in the opposite direction, he marched into the mayor's office. He boldly proposed, "If you assign me as special deputy city marshal, I'll take care of those fellas shooting up this place." The mayor, frustrated with the situation, sized up the tall, well-built man and then handed him a badge. He said, "All right—get busy! Let's see what you can do about these troublemakers! I'll back you up!" With that, Jim went to work, and by that evening, Telluride's jail was full of hooligans, ruffians, and loudmouthed thugs. The town was unusually quiet that night; the mayor breathed a sigh of relief, and Telluride's citizens ventured out safely.

Although he was usually armed and could draw his revolver with lightning speed, Jim didn't use his gun to bring peace to Telluride. When he confronted a drunk or hoodlum who reached for his six-shooter, Clark just walloped him with his fists, knocked him down, and relieved him of his weapon. The mayor and city council members were so impressed with his efficiency that they promptly named Jim Clark the new Telluride marshal and sent the previous coward on his way.

In the winter of 1890, Doc Shoes met Jim Clark, a man he'd heard a lot about. Jim was chasing a thief who'd stolen a horse in Telluride and was believed to be hiding in the Gunnison area. Clark sought the help of the widely respected Sheriff Shores, and the two lawmen combed the countryside for the horse thief. Finally, Doc tracked him to an outhouse, knocked on the door and ordered, "Open up now!" When there was no response, Doc threatened, "Open up, or I'll kick this door in!" A voice from inside yelled, "You'd better not!" The lawman replied, "I'm Doc Shores, the sheriff, and I'm arresting you for stealing a horse in Telluride!"

There was a snarl. "Go to h—! I'll come out when I'm ready." Doc drew his gun and kicked the outhouse door open. The man inside threw up his hands but still refused to come out. The sheriff grabbed the man by the collar and began dragging him out when Clark came running up, laughing. "I've got to hand it to you, Doc! This is one horse thief you really caught with his pants down!"

In turn for helping him capture the horse thief, Clark joined Doc in tracking down and rounding up a ring of rustlers who'd been sealing cattle from Gunnison ranchers. These shared efforts to catch outlaws were the beginning of a friendship between the two men. Shores wrote, "In spite of his serious faults, Clark had many admirable qualities which I learned to appreciate as I got to know him." Over the coming years, when Shores was in Telluride, he always visited Jim at his cabin, which was hidden in the willows on the outskirts of town.

In the evening, Doc walked with Jim as he patrolled the streets of Telluride, keeping a watchful eye out for troublemakers. If there was a noisy free-for-all in a saloon, Clark quickly put a stop to it. He never drank and had no use for "ladies of the evening." He'd look in on the elderly residents of Telluride to check on their welfare and help with heavy chores. He often bought materials and made repairs on their flimsy shacks. When a destitute family desperately needed money for food and medical care, Clark "loaned" them a generous amount that could be repaid when they "struck it rich."

Jim Clark was fond of dogs and children, and the big, colorful marshal was a town celebrity, always followed by groups of youngsters as he made his rounds. He often stopped and talked with these young admirers, who beamed at this attention. One afternoon, when Doc joined his friend on town patrol, Clark noticed a young boy who was struggling to carry two large buckets of water up a steep hill to a cabin. He hurried to the youngster and asked, "Can I give you a hand?" Pleased at the help of the

Main Street, Telluride, 1890s. The original San Miguel Valley Bank sign is visible on left side. *Telluride Historical Museum.*

illustrious lawman, the boy handed over a bucket. The pair plodded up the hill to the dilapidated cabin, where the boy's widowed mother took in laundry to support her family. Clark solved the boy's water problem when he bought an old work horse and outfitted it with a harness and barrel that could be filled in the creek. The horse hauled the water up the hill to the laundry woman's shack every day, while Clark kept the old horse fed with plenty of hay and grain.

Clark saved Doc's life in 1894, when he was working as a special investigator for the Rio Grande Southern Railroad. Doc had arrested Bill Schafer, the popular ringleader of a large gang of outlaws. Schafer had held up the Mancos Train Station, and his trial was held in Cortez, Montezuma County. Outlaws from southwestern Colorado and northwestern New Mexico rode in to help Schafer any way they could. Most camped in a canyon a few miles from Cortez and came to town every day armed to the teeth to fill the courtroom. Since Doc was the main witness for the state, it was rumored that "his life wasn't worth a dime."

When Clark heard that Doc Shores was in danger, he headed for Cortez with his friend Marmaduke, who'd ridden with him in Quantrill's guerrillas. They took the train from Telluride to the end of the line, rented horses, and rode to Cortez. They arrived in the middle of the night, and Doc was surprised when they walked into the courtroom the following morning. Both men were carrying a rifle and wore a six-shooter on each hip.

Clark had been tipped off that the defendant's friends intended to shoot Doc to prevent him from testifying. He was well known among the outlaws, and it got around that he and his friend had come to Cortez to protect Doc and prevent gunplay. No one wanted to tangle with the deadly guns of Doc's famous escort Jim Clark. Doc wrote in his memoir, "Their presence had a healthy effect on the threatening crowd and dampened the ardor of the gunmen who intended to cause trouble." Doc later learned that Clark's presence had disrupted a genuine assassination plot against him. Doc Shores always said, "It meant a lot to me to see at least two who were on my side." The judge asked Doc to have his well-armed friends come to court every day to maintain order while Doc testified. They accompanied him wherever he went, and Doc was certain that he'd have been shot in the back without their protection.

Doc's testimony was the deciding factor in the case, and Schafer was sentenced to fourteen years in prison. Clark and Marmaduke rode out of Cortez with Doc, the Montezuma County sheriff, and Schafer. They were followed at a distance by a group of outlaws who wisely decided not to start

Telluride Valley floor. *Photograph by Tom Williams.*

trouble. When they reached the train depot in Dolores, Doc was accosted by a drunken cowboy who protested about the leg irons that were kept on the prisoner. He finally stopped the harassment when the lawman threatened to put him in chains, too.

While waiting for the train in a nearby hotel lobby, Doc was called to the telegraph office. As Doc stepped out on the street, his Winchester ready, the cowboy came out of a nearby saloon with a six-shooter in his hand. He'd boosted his courage with a few more drinks. Jim Clark came running and warned, "Watch out, Doc! This feller is gunning for you!" Clark raised his gun to shoot the troublemaker, but the Montezuma County sheriff yelled, "Don't shoot! Don't kill him!" Clark asked, "Why not? He's going to kill Shores!" The cowboy backed off but reappeared as Doc was leaving the telegraph office. He and Clark kept their guns on him so he couldn't shoot them in the back as they carefully moved backward into the hotel lobby. When Shores asked the sheriff why he didn't arrest the drunk, the sheriff replied, embarrassed, "I can't. He's my deputy."

The train pulled in about then, and they hustled the prisoner to the depot with the cowboy on their heels, hurling insults. Clark had enough and quietly removed his coat, saying, "If I can't shoot the b— I'll knock the s— out of him!" Shores knew that a few blows from a powerful fighter like Clark could be fatal to the smaller man, so he grabbed his friend's arm. "Let him go," he said. He reminded Clark that if he did serious damage, they'd have to return to testify before a coroner's jury and deal with a lot of red tape.

They got their prisoner on the train for the long journey to the Territorial Prison at Canon City. To be safe, Doc, Clark, and the sheriff stood on the back platform, rifles ready, as they chugged out of Dolores. If the drunk had taken a pot shot at them, they would have let him have it. Doc said, "It was with a sigh of relief that I left southwestern Colorado where I'd spent so many months tracking down, arresting and convicting the Mancos station robber." He continued, "I will always feel that I would not have gotten out of that country alive if it hadn't been for Jim Clark."

The last few years that Clark was the Telluride city marshal, he worked during the day, and a man named MacDuff was hired as the night marshal. Since no one had been tough enough to handle the marshal's job, the rumors about Clark's criminal activities had been ignored by the city council. But now that MacDuff showed he could do the job, Clark was fired. He was furious and threatened to kill the members of the city council for "15 cents apiece or two for a quarter." The city clerk and a judge were seriously concerned about him and wrote to Doc Shores, asking him to come to Telluride. "You have more influence on him than any other man alive," they said in the hopes Shores could persuade his friend to leave town before someone was hurt.

Shores took the train to Telluride and spent the night at Clark's cabin, where they reminisced about happier times. Then Doc said, "Jim you've got the new lawman over a barrel. They won't try to arrest you or have it out with you openly because they know you're too much for them. Their only alternative is to shoot you in the back or resign, and we both know they won't resign. If I were in your place, I'd get out of town before I was bushwacked.... Your life is in real danger."

Clark finally agreed to leave Telluride and asked Doc to write a letter of recommendation, since he wanted to continue working in law enforcement. Doc assured his friend that he'd do it because he would like to see Clark as a lawman "in a place far away from here." Shores said, "That was the last time I saw Jim Clark alive." He returned to Gunnison and immediately composed a letter of recommendation, praising Clark as "one of the greatest peace officers that I have ever known."

A day later, on August 7, 1895, Doc received a telegram from the county clerk in Telluride: "Jim Clark killed last night. Come if you can." Doc took the first train to Telluride, and the clerk and county judge met him at the depot that night. They told him what had happened. On the previous night, Clark was walking down Main Street with a man known as Mexican Sam. As they passed the Colombo Saloon, a shot rang out, and Clark grabbed his chest, saying, "I'm shot. Go for a doctor!" Then he walked out into the street and peered up at the rooftops of nearby buildings, looking for the shooter. He stumbled back to the sidewalk and collapsed in front of Agee's Barber Shop. A large crowd quickly gathered, and Clark was carried to a nearby cabin, where the doctor examined his wound. He might have survived if the bullet hadn't severed an artery and caused him to bleed to death. The blood-soaked letter of recommendation from Doc was tucked into his breast pocket. Shores said sadly, "Clark could never have been killed in an open fight: someone had to ambush him." He praised his friend saying, "Jim Clark was tough, brave, and the most fearless man that I ever knew. I suppose many mean things will be said about him now that he's dead."

All of Telluride turned out for Jim Clark's funeral: the mayor and city council, businessmen and shopkeepers, gamblers and miners. There were crowds of children and old people whom he'd often helped. There were many he'd befriended or given a helping hand to as he brought law and order to the town. Jim Clark was buried in the Grand Army plot of the Lone Tree Cemetery with the Union soldiers, even though he'd fought for the Confederacy. A marble monument was placed on his grave, which the children covered with bouquets of wildflowers. After the funeral, Doc went to Clark's cabin, lifted the floorboard, removed his coat, hat, and whiskers and burned them. In his *Memoirs*, Doc said, "It was the last favor that I could bestow on a loyal friend, who like most of us, had a lot of good in him as well as a lot of bad."

Author's note: Doc Shores wrote in Memoirs of a Lawman, *"In those days, there was often just a thin line between a lawman and an outlaw. For example, Wyatt Earp was a highwayman even while he was marshal of Tombstone. Wild Bill Hickock was a natural killer and often shot men down for minor offenses without giving them a fair draw." Shores continued, "These lawmen and their like, of which I knew many, played a major role in the winning of the West. Their good deeds outshone their bad. So it was with Jim Clark." Shores continued, "As a peace officer I soon learned that if one is going to be successful in his work, he must have friends on both sides of the law."*

8

THE STOCKTON-ESKRIDGE GANG AND THE SAN JUAN COUNTY WAR

Porter "Port" Stockton killed a man when he was twelve years old "for calling him a liar by shooting the top of his head off," reported a January 10, 1881 article in *The Durango Weekly Record.* There are no other details, but according to those who knew young Porter, this was just the first of a long string of assaults in which he killed or maimed many men. Porter had a short fuse and a chip on his shoulder, and he was often in trouble. There's no doubt he became a remorseless, cold-hearted killer. He was supported in these deeds by his younger brother, Ike, who was usually mild-mannered and agreeable. The boys were born into a typically Southern white family, poor and uneducated. They migrated to Texas after it entered the Union in 1845. Their early years were full of hardship, and after his father and oldest brother died, Port was left to support the family.

In February 1871, a grand jury indicted Porter for assault with intent to kill after he threatened a friend during an argument. He had a good lawyer, who got him released on bail, so he wasted no time leaving Texas for good. Port spent time in the saddle, driving cattle to Kansas cow towns, where he went on drunken, violent rampages. He reportedly killed a man in Dodge City and shot another in Ellsworth, Kansas, in 1873. In Wichita, he tried to kill Wyatt Earp, but the gunman shot his weapon out of his hand. Port joined cattle drives that herded the first Texas longhorns up the Goodnight-Loving Trail to northern New Mexico. Ike soon followed, and the brothers spent the next few years in the border region of northeastern New Mexico and around Trinidad in southeastern Colorado.

Port shot and killed Deputy Antonio Arcibia in Cimarron, New Mexico, on New Year's Day 1876, when the deputy accused him of making advances toward his wife. Stockton was indicted in March, but he quickly skipped over the border to Trinidad. He was arrested here by Sheriff Barela and returned to custody in Cimarron in early September. On September 16, Ike visited Port in his jail cell, and the two men surprised and overcame the jailer. They tore up sheets to bind his hands and feet, tied him to the cot, locked him in the cell, and raced out of town. Hours later, when the jailer was discovered and freed, the sheriff didn't even try to pursue the Stocktons, saying, "It was just too late."

Port stayed clear of Cimarron and Colfax County for three years after his jail escape and started a small ranch in Otero. This was the first railroad camp and settlement created by the Santa Fe Railroad as it laid tracks into New Mexico. The wild camp, six miles south of Raton, attracted Doc Holliday and the notorious horse thieves Hurricane Bill Martin and brothers Bill and Ed Withers. Port was running cattle nearby and liked to dash through Otero with his cowboys, shooting and yelling. In June 1879, he was arrested and fined by Hurricane Bill, the unlikely city marshal. Port shot Ed Withers, Bill's popular friend, and then killed his deputy. Once again, he wasn't indicted for the crimes.

By 1880, Otero had become too hot for Port so he packed up his wife and three daughters, rounded up his cattle, and headed for Animas City, Colorado. His brother, Ike, owned a small ranch there and was well established in this small farming community in southwestern Colorado. Port posed as a prosperous stockman and impressed the town's citizens so much that he was made city marshal.

Inclined to pull his gun at any slight, he shot and wounded a man named Hart for no reason. A few days after this murder, a drunken Port wandered into the town barbershop and demanded a shave. The Black barber accidentally nicked him during the shave, infuriating Port. He pulled his six-shooter and whacked the barber over the head. Then Port chased him down the street before taking a few shots at him. A bullet grazed the barber's head and knocked him down, inflicting a minor wound. Port pounced on the barber and beat the poor man's head with his gun. The July 25, 1880 *La Plata Miner* described Port's attack as a "dastardly act." Unwilling to tolerate this, the mayor of Animas City raised a posse, who arrested Port and confined him in his house with his gun and a horse nearby. Port escaped and raced out of town, and the mayor was congratulated for getting rid of their troublesome marshal without bloodshed. Port quickly

The Stockton-Eskridge Gang in Durango, 1880. *Left to right*: Byson Eskridge, Harg Eskridge, Port Stockton and Ike Stockton. *La Plata County Historical Society*.

moved his wife and three daughters into a cabin near Bloomfield, New Mexico, and returned to ranching.

Eighty large cattle operations in northern New Mexico joined together and organized the Farmington Stockmen's Protective Association and began driving small ranchers out of the area. The *Dolores News* of Rico, Colorado and the *Durango Record* railed against the highhanded New Mexico organization's tactics, calling it the "Farmington mob." The mob accused the Stocktons of rustling, driving their cattle across the border into Colorado, and selling them to the army camp near Animas City. The Simmons family of Farmington and the powerful Coe clan became bitter enemies of the Stocktons.

Dow Eskridge had been farming in Kansas until 1873, when he decided to come west. He settled in the San Luis Valley of Colorado, where he farmed and raised cattle. Eventually, he moved his herd to the grasslands of the lower Animas Valley, near Farmington. The New Mexican cattlemen did not welcome him because their herds were already crowded together, and they were running out of open range. When Dow was joined by his brothers, Harg and Dyson, and cowboy Jim Garrett, the mob made plans to push them out. Dyson and Harg joined forces with Ike and Port Stockton.

On Christmas Eve 1880, several of Port's friends—Dyson Eskridge, Jim Garrett, and some cowboys who'd had too much Christmas cheer—crashed a holiday dance that was held by the Farmington mob in Bloomfield. They were rebuffed, and there was a gunfight. Two mob cowboys were killed, and Eskridge was wounded. The mob was enraged and offered a $1,000 reward for Eskridge and Garrett "dead or alive." There was increased hostility toward Ike and Port, even though they weren't involved.

The *Durango Record* reported that "the best citizens—all members of the Farmington mob—ransacked the house of Garrett and Dyson Eskridge, stole anything of value, then burned the house, and took their horses and cattle."

Two weeks later, on January 4, 1881, two members of the Farmington mob rode up to Port's cabin. When he answered the door, they began a friendly conversation just as five others rode past. Those men suddenly whirled around and fired at Port, while the two men at his door drew their revolvers and shot him, too. Port toppled over, dead. His wife, Emily, ran outside with a rifle, and the two men shot her and then galloped off. Emily was badly wounded, and their three young children were left alone in the cabin until a friend arrived to help.

The partisan New Mexican newspapers published their versions of Port's murder. Some characterized it as an act of "community improvement," while another repeated Port's boast that he'd killed nineteen men. "It is very gratifying to write the obituary of such a desperado. He died with his boots on." Emily survived the attack but was seriously injured, and Ike assumed responsibility for her and the children. He swore to avenge his brother's murder, and the San Juan County War began in earnest. This conflict raged for two years, involving local newspapers and the governors of Colorado and New Mexico, took a number of lives, and made national headlines.

Ike recruited additional cowboys for his gang: young Bert Wilkinson, Kid Thomas, and Charley Allison. Shortly after this, two of the men who'd shot Port were ambushed and killed on the La Plata River. The newspapers took sides with the *La Plata Miner* of Silverton, accusing the victims of shooting first. A grand jury in New Mexico indicted Ike Stockton, Harg Eskridge, Jim Garrett, and seven others in the gang for the murders. Governor Lew Wallace of New Mexico offered a reward for the capture of nine men in the Stockton Gang.

In January 1881, two weeks after Port's murder, three members of the New Mexico mob accosted a one-armed man named Welfoot and hauled him off to Farmington for a mock trial in a kangaroo court. He was found guilty of publicly condemning the killers for shooting Port's wife. Welfoot was ordered to leave the county in ten days or be shot on sight. He wasn't intimidated by this threat and remained on his homestead; the Farmington bunch didn't carry out their threats.

On April 17, 1881, about thirty members of the Farmington mob rode across the state line and took up positions on a high mesa directly above Durango. They began firing at the saloons lining Railroad Avenue, where the Stockton Gang was drinking and carousing. Ike and the cowboys rushed out of the saloon, guns drawn, and returned gunfire as Durango's citizens scrambled for cover. The gunfight went on for over an hour until both sides ran out of ammunition, and the mob withdrew. Despite the intensity of this shootout, no one was killed, and there were only a few minor casualties. The April 16, 1881 *Dolores News* and *Durango Record* condemned the mob for attacking Durango, endangering women and children, and called for their arrest.

The Durango gunfight and the San Juan County War earned banner headlines in newspapers across the country. The April 2, 1881 *Daily Nevada State Journal* of Reno reported that "the whole section of the country around Rio Arabia [*sic*], New Mexico, is in a state of nervous excitement and terror. The cause of the terror is Ike Stockton, who with his brother, Port, have for years been depredating [*sic*] through New Mexico and Texas, murdering and stealing." The *Wellsboro Pennsylvania Agitato*r of April 19 noted, "Stockton's gang of desperadoes are ruling Rio Arriba County with terror, robbery, and murder." The *Denver Republican* of April 14 reported that Colorado desperadoes were leading raiding parties to steal cattle and kill cowboys around Farmington. On April 16, the *Santa Fe New Mexican* declared that Stockton's gang had stolen fifteen horses and a herd of cattle and driven them back to Durango.

As threats of violence increased, Governor Wallace of New Mexico ordered Adjutant General Frost to take two infantry companies of the state militia, the San Juan Guards, to Rio Arriba County to capture Stockton and his gang. If Stockton's men entered New Mexico, murder warrants were to be served on them. Frost promised that Governor Wallace would declare a state of insurrection and call for U.S. troops to come to New Mexico. The battle of words between the two states' newspapers continued, filled with accusations and threats, lies and exaggerations, and testimonials about the sterling characters of each side's participants. This kept the two factions stirred up and agitated the citizens of New Mexico and Colorado.

The *Dolores News*, which was published in Rico, Colorado, continued defending the Stockton-Eskridge faction. The Farmington bunch refused to allow Dow Eskridge to gather his cattle from their winter pasture in Rio Arriba County and drive them to Colorado until Ike Stockton was arrested.

An iconic 1890s scene of downtown Durango, where the Utes would trade and camp. Note the Strater Hotel in the far upper left corner. *La Plata County Historical Society.*

This nonsense created another flurry of newsprint when Governor Pitkin of Colorado refused to hand over Ike and his gang.

The August 11, 1881 *Denver Republic* carried an interview with Ike Stockton, in which he insisted he'd never stolen any cattle or killed anyone. The reporter described Ike as a "pleasant faced, mild mannered gentleman, standing five-feet-four-inches, weighing 164 pounds, and compactly built. Ike, twenty-nine years old, sported a goatee and mustache, was well-dressed with gold studs in his shirt cuffs and a silver watch chain draped cross his vest." The reporter concluded, "He was anything but a ruffian."

The same reporter described Dyson Eskridge as being "a tall, rawboned young man…dark complexioned with a fine black mustache, heavy jawbone, and a large, prominent chin." He said Dyson was "tight-lipped, spoke only when spoken to and seldom laughed." He also said Eskridge was always alert and was the "gang's crack shot." The reporter commented that Dyson seemed "the most cold-blooded and naturally desperate member of the gang." He observed that Dyson didn't command the respect that Ike Stockton did. He commented that he'd seen Dyson shoot at a man as he crossed the street in Durango just to "see how near he could come."

The violence continued as Tom Lacey, a cattleman, was gunned down by "Big Dan" Holland, a man he'd hired to find out who was stealing horses and cattle from his New Mexico ranch. A few days later, Eskridge killed Kid White, a young desperado, after he received a tip that the Kid was out to get him for the reward Governor Wallace had put on his head months earlier.

On August 22, Stockton Gang members Bert Wilkinson, Jim Catron, and a Black youth known as the "Copper Colored Kid" or "Kid Thomas" robbed a Durango saloon. The following day, Dyson Eskridge joined them, and they headed to Silverton, a bustling silver camp in the San Juan Mountains. A popular saloon owner, Clayton Ogsbury, had recently been appointed as the new city marshal.

On August 24, Sheriff Hunter of La Plata County, Colorado, sent word to Marshal Ogsbury that he was leaving Durango with warrants for the arrest of Kid Thomas and Bert Wilkinson for the saloon robbery. Ogsbury waited for him until 10:00 p.m. and then went to bed. Hunter arrived in Silverton after midnight and woke Ogsbury. The sheriff and the marshal, accompanied by Deputy Hodges, headed for the Diamond Saloon, where Wilkinson, Thomas, and Catron were drinking. Ogsbury saw someone lurking in the shadows near the saloon, but before he could say anything or draw his gun, he was shot. He dropped to the street, mortally wounded,

Left: Silverton Marshal David Clayton "Clate" Ogsbury. *Photograph of a sketch at Silverton Museum; photograph by Tom Williams.*

Right: Kid Thomas's grave marker, Silverton Cemetery. *Photograph by Les Clements.*

as Hodges rushed to his side. Seeing that it was too late to help Ogsbury, Hodges ran for cover, and Sheriff Hunter disappeared. Wilkinson, Eskridge, and Thomas fled on foot, leaving their horses behind in the livery stable.

Silverton's citizens quickly organized a posse to search for the culprits. They found Kid Thomas hiding behind the Grand Imperial Hotel and jailed him. The posse combed the rugged country around Silverton, but Wilkinson and Eskridge were gone. The county commissioners offered a $2,500 reward for the arrest of either Dyson Eskridge or Bert Wilkinson. Silverton's citizens were furious that their popular marshal had been murdered and that Sheriff Hunter couldn't be found. A vigilante committee jerked Kid Thomas out of his cell that night and hanged the sixteen-year-old from a rafter in the woodshed behind the jail.

The posse scoured the mountains surrounding Silverton, and wanted posters were plastered across Colorado, Arizona, and New Mexico. Clate Ogsbury was a member of the Rocky Mountain Detective Association, which sent Captain C.A. Hawley, a well-known sleuth, to help with the manhunt.

A few days after Clayton Ogsbury was buried in Silverton's Hillside Cemetery, Ike Stockton was deputized by Sheriff Hunter of La Plata County. He and Marion Cook, a deputy marshal, left Durango on August 17 and headed into the San Juan Mountains. On September 1, Ike Stockton rode into Durango and announced that he and Cook had captured Bert Wilkinson. He was making arrangements for payment of the reward. After he collected the reward, he said the prisoner would be turned over to

Silverton authorities. When it was dark, Cook brought Wilkinson to Animas City, where he was confined and held under guard in a hotel.

A reporter from the *Durango Southwest* newspaper interviewed Bert Wilkinson at the hotel. He admitted that he felt responsible for Ogsbury's murder. He was upset by the lynching of his friend, "the Kid," and called it "a foul murder." He said his greatest fear was of being lynched by people from Silverton. The reporter said there were several guards "armed to the teeth" protecting Wilkinson.

On September 3, Stockton and Cook took Wilkinson to a point about thirty miles from Silverton to meet Sheriff Thornilly of San Juan County. The sheriff handed $2,500 to Ike and took charge of Wilkinson. A twelve-man posse escorted him to the Silverton Jail. Flora Pyle, Wilkinson's older sister, came to Silverton and begged anyone who'd listen to see that her brother had a fair trial. The sheriff told her that Bert was going to be hanged without a trial and that she should leave town. He promised that her brother's body would be sent to her. Flora spent time with Bert at the jail, and left Silverton in tears on Sunday. On Sunday night September 4, a group of masked men entered the jail, overpowered the guards, and hanged Bert Wilkinson in his cell. His body was discovered hours later, and it was placed in a coffin and sent to his sister.

An early photograph believed to be of Bert Wilkinson. *Public domain.*

Six days after Bert Wilkinson was hanged, the September 10, 1881 *Dolores News* printed a lengthy statement from his sister, Flora Pyle, that illustrated Ike Stockton's treachery. She said Ike had come to her home on Sunday evening, August 28, to warn her brother that a search party from Silverton was looking for him. Bert Wilkinson and Dyson Eskridge were not at Flora's home when Stockton arrived. He decided to wait for them and spent the night at Flora's, sleeping in an outbuilding. Late that night, Bert and Dyson Eskridge stumbled into Flora's house, hungry and exhausted after fleeing from Silverton. Dyson had lost his boots and was barefoot. They were "overjoyed" when Flora told them Ike was at her house. In the morning, after they ate breakfast, Bert and Dyson Eskridge rode off with Ike on horses that Flora supplied.

While Flora spent time with Bert at the Silverton Jail, he told her what had happened after he and Dyson left her home with Ike. She said,

> *They met Cook at a rendezvous, and then Ike Stockton left with Dyson. He returned alone saying they would meet Harg Eskridge and Dyson with fresh horses. Bert stood up, leaving his gun where he'd been sitting. Stockton immediately ordered, "Throw up your hands!" Bert thought he was joking and started laughing. He asked, "Do you mean it?" When he saw Ike's face, he knew this wasn't a joke. Stockton snarled, "Yes, I do mean it—money is what makes men in this country." Bert said sadly, "You've got the drop on me Ike, but I'd rather you killed me."*

Editor Jones assured his readers that he'd known Flora Pyle for years, and he believed that her account of Bert's capture was accurate. In his opinion, Bert Wilkinson was simply "a misguided boy, encouraged in his misdeeds by Stockton and his companions…the treachery of Stockton in delivering up his comrade to be hung simply for a monied consideration solely, is an action which caused the loss of all the friends he had." Jones said Bert's capture was a good thing, "but the means are detestable." He added that, in his opinion, "the capturer is more detestable than the captured."

Charles Jones had always defended Ike Stockton in the *Dolores News*, and he'd covered the murder of Clayton Ogsbury, a personal friend. He described nineteen-year-old Bert Wilkinson as "an overgrown boy, generous and good of heart, even at the time of his death. His career of crime had been of very short duration." He lamented that the lives of two fine young men had been snuffed out unnecessarily. In an editorial, Jones said Wilkinson had been misled by "evil associations," and although his crime couldn't be excused, "the man who'd captured him, Ike Stockton, had a black heart." Jones wrote that Stockton's treachery in dealing with Wilkinson, a longtime friend and compatriot, had opened his eyes.

To further illustrate Stockton's greed, Jones told the story of Tom Radigan, a member of the gang, who had been shot in a gunfight with the Farmington mob months before. Ike took him to Fort Lewis for medical care, and his wounded leg was eventually amputated. After delivering Radigan to Fort Lewis, Ike Stockton arranged to have him arrested and turned over to the Farmington mob. Then he collected the reward the mob was offering. Jones added that the only reason Ike Stockton didn't turn in Dyson Eskridge was that he was afraid his brother Harg would kill him.

Newspapers denounced Ike Stockton's treachery and predicted that Durango would become "too warm" for him. La Plata County Sheriff Hunt resigned and was replaced by Barney Watson. On September 26, Ike Stockton and Marion Cook were arrested in Durango by Sheriff Watson. He had a warrant from the governor of Texas for Cook's arrest, and he was quickly taken into custody. Then Watson and his deputies went after Stockton with a warrant from Governor Wallace of New Mexico for his arrest for murder. When the deputies approached Ike, he pulled his gun, and both lawmen fired, hitting him in the leg. Ike tumbled to the ground and was quickly disarmed. Stockton and Cook were loaded into a wagon and taken to the smelter across the Animas River, which was safer from vigilantes than the jail.

The bullets had shattered Stockton's thigh and broken a bone in his lower leg. Seven doctors worked on his leg, but it had to be amputated. Ike died several hours later on September 26, 1881, from shock and loss of blood. The *Colorado Springs Gazette* reported, "The poor wife and her two children were present at the death bed." Ike Stockton was buried a day later in the Animas City Cemetery.

Dyson Eskridge, twenty-one, escaped to Arizona and was killed in Yuma in 1881. Harg left Colorado and returned to his childhood home in Pennsylvania. The San Juan County War faded after the deaths of Ike and Porter Stockton and Dyson Eskridge and the departure of Harg.

9

QUEEN ANN BASSETT BATTLES THE CATTLE KINGS

Sam Bassett didn't find gold in California, but he discovered Brown's Park in Colorado. When he was exploring the West, his glowing letters home to his brother, Herb, were full of the potential and possibilities he saw in this remote corner of northwestern Colorado. Back in post–Civil War Arkansas, the future was grim, so Herb and his wife, Elizabeth, decided their future looked brighter in the new state of Colorado.

The Bassetts arrived in Brown's Park in 1877 and set to work. Herb built their first home, a two-room log cabin with a dirt floor and a sod roof. Then he put down a wooden floor, built cupboards and shelves, and made a table and comfortable chairs from birch saplings. He planted an apple orchard and piped water from a nearby spring to water the young trees. Elizabeth did her best to make a comfortable home for them and their two young children. She said she felt an immediate connection to the valley, with its rolling hills that sloped down to the Green River, and were fringed with willows and cottonwood trees. Elizabeth said this valley, often referred to as Brown's Hole, "should never be called a hole because it was a lovely park."

On May 12, 1878, Ann Bassett became the first white baby born in Brown's Park. Her sister, Josie, was four years old and her brother, Sam, was two years younger. The Bassett family grew when Elbert arrived in 1880, and George came in 1884. Their father, Herb, was a scholar and a musician, and he purchased an organ in Rock Springs, Wyoming, and hauled it home in a wagon. The Bassett home was filled with music, good books, and plans for the future. As more people established homesteads in

Ann Bassett, queen of the outlaws, circa 1904. *Denver Public Library Digital Collections [Z-153].*

Brown's Park, the small settlement grew and was awarded a post office. Herb served as postmaster and eventually became the justice of the peace and a county commissioner. Since the couple decided to raise cattle, Herb built a barn and corrals. They bought cattle to develop a herd, planned their pastures, and hired a cowhand to help Elizabeth, who managed the entire operation.

Some settlers built their herds by purchasing additional cattle or by rounding up unbranded calves, called "slicks." These animals were quickly branded and added to the growing herd. Matt Warner, a cowboy and a rustler who started a ranch in Brown's Park, described this practice in his book *The Last of the Bandit Riders*: "Cattle ranged far and wide. The owners couldn't keep the growing stock all branded. If one person didn't brand an unbranded critter, the next person would. This kind of condition always led to competition in branding that pushed most of the cattlemen and cowboys over the line in the direction of plain cattle stealing and led to all kinds of trouble." Dick Dunham wrote in his book *Flaming Gorge Country*, "Technically, rustling cattle was a felony offense," and with very few exceptions, "everybody…in Brown's Park engaged in it." Elizabeth Bassett decided she'd do a little rustling, too, and before long, the Bassetts had an impressive herd of cattle. Elizabeth hired cowboys Isom Dart, Matt Rash, Angus McDougal, and Jim McKnight, who were often referred to as the "Bassett Gang."

Historians agree that Isom Dart's background is unclear and full of contradictions, starting with his birthplace: Was he born in Arkansas in 1849 or in Texas in 1858? Texas did not end slavery until June 19, 1863, so was Dart born into slavery like many other Black cowboys? There is also the question of his name: Was he born Ned Huddleston and later switched his name to Isom Dart? The 1870 Texas census includes a "twelve-year-old Isom Dart" and three siblings. His father, Cyrus Dart, was listed as a farmer, and his mother, Indiana, was listed as a twenty-five-year-old who "kept the house." Isom, who was fluent in Spanish, picked up the language as a boy living in a diverse Texas community of Hispanic, Black, and Native American people. He began riding horses when he was very young, and as a teenager, he could manage difficult horses and wild mustangs. When he was about sixteen, he was hired by the Texas trail driver Ab Blocker for his first cattle drive. He became an outstanding cowboy and had plenty of work on drives.

After the Civil War, Texas was overrun with wild longhorns, and small ranchers began building herds of these feral animals to start their cattle businesses. Every year, they'd drive at least one herd to eastern markets or to a railroad shipping depot in Missouri or Kansas. Dart saw that Texas ranchers needed plenty of horses for the task, and he knew where to get them. In South Texas, daring cowboys crossed the Rio Grande River and ventured into Mexico, where there were plenty of wild mustangs. They rounded up the mustangs and drove them back across the river into Texas, where they sold them for a profit. If mustangs weren't around, they'd steal a tame herd from a Mexican rancher. Cowboys like Dart, who were skilled bronc busters, were hired to break these wild mustangs and train them to be smart, tough cow ponies.

Dart joined Tip Gault's gang of rustlers, stealing horses and cattle, but this venture turned out badly. When one of the outlaws was killed by a fierce mustang, his grave was dug by his comrades. As they dug, they were suddenly blasted by a hail of bullets. A posse had tracked them down, and every one of the rustlers was killed—except Dart, who jumped into the open grave and played dead. Satisfied that they'd eliminated their problem, the posse rode off, leaving the outlaws' bodies scattered about. Dart eventually climbed out of the grave and stole a horse from a nearby ranch, but he was spotted by the rancher, who shot him in the leg as he galloped off. The wound was serious, and Dart became so weak from blood loss that he fell off his horse. He was unconscious, lying by the trail, when a cowboy found him and managed to stop the bleeding. The cowboy loaded Dart on a horse, took him to a safe place and nursed him back to health.

When he recovered, Dart joined a drive to take cattle from Texas to stock a new ranch in Wyoming Territory. Matt Rash, another Texas cowboy, was the trail boss, and they became friends. Dart and Rash decided to stay in Wyoming, where they were both hired by the large Middlesex Ranch. Dart was a wrangler and bronc buster, and Rash was the foreman. Isom Dart was a tall, well-built Black cowboy, an expert with a rifle and lasso. He could handle wild mustangs and was known for his ability to tame outlaw horses that were "as bad as any ever wore hair."

The large Middlesex Land and Cattle Company was started in the late 1870s by a man named Clay, who was financed by Boston investors. Clay was determined to seize the grazing land of Brown's Park and swore he'd

Isom Dart studio portrait. *J. Green, circa 1870–80; Denver Public Library Digital Collections [X-21560].*

"buy all the little fellows out or drive 'em out of the country!" Disgusted with Clay's tactics, Matt Rash and Isom Dart quit Middlesex. Rash was hired as foreman of Tim McKinney's Circle K Ranch near Brown's Park, and Dart went to work for Elizabeth Bassett. Rash saw that McKinney was being pressured by Clay and was disappointed when his boss finally gave up and sold his ranch. Rash headed for the Bassett ranch, where he was welcomed by Elizabeth, who needed top hands.

This photograph of Matt Rash was taken shortly before his death, circa 1900. It is the only known photograph of him. *Museum of Northwest Colorado.*

Work at the Bassett ranch was divided, with Herb handling the paperwork and finances and educating the children. Elizabeth managed the growing cattle operation, and Dart, in addition to his cowboy work, often helped out by cooking meals, taking care of the laundry, and doing household chores. He was treated like a member of the family and taught the Bassett children how to ride and use a lasso. Thanks to Dart's lessons, Eb Bassett, Ann's younger brother, became one of the area's best ropers. Ann and Josie could rope and ride with the best cowhands, but when they were teenagers, they were sent to finishing school to complete their education. Both girls preferred cowboying and were always glad to get back to the ranch.

Matt Rash was promoted to foreman by Elizabeth, and he and Dart saw an opportunity to eventually own their own spreads. They saved their wages and bought cattle while they continued to work for the Bassetts. Matt acquired a piece of land with a stream about two miles west of the Bassett ranch and built a log cabin. He grazed his slowly growing herd nearby. Dart broke mustangs and trained them to become cow ponies, which earned him extra money to buy cattle. He built a cabin on his piece of land on Cold Spring Mountain and continued working for Elizabeth. Both men were close friends of the Bassett family.

Elizabeth Bassett helped organize the Brown's Park Cattle Association, and Matt Rash was elected its first president. Clay was still trying to move his Middlesex cattle into Brown's Park, so the association made a plan to stop him. They moved several flocks of sheep to the entrance of the park and kept them there. Sheep are known for overgrazing and chewing grass down to the ground; they destroy forage and cause erosion. When the sheep were eventually moved, Clay drove his cattle in, but there was nothing left for them to eat. The Middlesex herd suffered and grew thin in 1884–85 and was totally wiped out by the disastrous winter of 1886–87, which brought unusually frigid temperatures, numerous blizzards, and a record amount of snow.

Once Middlesex Ranch was gone, Ora Haley, the owner of the huge Two Bar Ranch, increased his efforts to push the small cattle operations out of Brown's Park. He hired Hi Bernard, an experienced Texas trail driver, to run his ranch while he pursued his political ambitions. When Wyoming was granted statehood in 1890, Haley served in the first state senate. Bernard developed the Two Bar into the largest ranch with the most cattle in Wyoming and western Colorado. It sprawled over twenty-five thousand acres in northern Colorado and fifty thousand acres in Wyoming. But this wasn't enough for Haley, who wanted the rich grazing land in Brown's Park, so he began moving herds into the eastern end of the valley along the Little Snake River.

Elizabeth Bassett and others didn't hesitate to slap their brands on some of Haley's unbranded calves. Wyoming cattlemen spread stories that everyone in Brown's Park was a rustler or horse thief, and outlaws were always welcome there. Of course, the park's residents denied this, and Ann Bassett was one of the most vocal. Years later, she wrote in her autobiography, "Rumors were circulated to the effect that not only were we cattle thieves ourselves, but we harbored outlaws and criminals from other states."

The park's remote location, with its ample amounts of water and grass, made it ideal for raising cattle and hiding out. Ann Zwinger described Brown's Park in her book *Run River Run* as "a more or less permanent hideout for many who found total honesty a personal encumbrance." Most of the people who lived in Brown's Park were considered law-abiding by their peers, but many did rustle cattle. They allowed known outlaws to live in Brown's Park periodically and use it as a hideout. Some residents, like the Bassetts, welcomed outlaws and provided shelter, food, and fresh horses.

Butch Cassidy and the Wild Bunch came to Brown's Park in the 1890s and often stayed in a hidden cabin near Charlie Crouse's ranch. Tired from hours in the saddle, riding over miles of rough country, they could rest, play poker, eat good food, and plan their next job. If a lawman or suspicious stranger showed up, Crouse sent someone to warn them. Brown's Park became one of their favorite hideouts, along with Robbers Roost in Utah and Wyoming's Hole in the Wall.

Few officers ventured over treacherous country to reach Brown's Park. Those who did knew their quarry could escape arrest by dashing across the border into Colorado, Utah, or Wyoming. The outlaws who haunted the region knew their geography well in this unusual patchwork of state territories and easily managed to elude their pursuers. The only lawmen whose authority could cross over state lines were the U.S. marshals, deputy U.S. marshals, and special deputies.

Ann Bassett reminisced about the Wild Bunch years later: "The young people of each group mingled and liked each other." She continued, "And let me say they had some cute boys with their outfit. It was a thrill to see Harry Longabaugh (The Sundance Kid) tall, blond & handsome." And photographs show that Ann and Josie were attractive young women who could ride, rope, and shoot.

Butch Cassidy divided his time between Crouse's hidden cabin and the Bassett ranch, where he was interested in Josie. She didn't reciprocate Butch's feelings, but fifteen-year-old Ann was definitely intrigued and became romantically involved with Cassidy. When he went to Wyoming Territorial Prison in 1894, she was romanced by Ben Kilpatrick of the gang. After Cassidy was paroled in 1896, he became entangled with both Josie and Ann. Despite this round-robin of romance between the Bassett girls and Wild Bunch outlaws, it didn't seem to cause much jealousy or animosity among the group. Ann Bassett maintained an off-and-on relationship with Cassidy for years. Josie was smitten by Elzy Lay, Butch's best friend, but took up with Will Carver and married Jim McKnight.

People congregated at the Bassetts' cabin for parties and to celebrate special events. Word was sent to everyone to mark their calendars when a dance or event was planned, and some even traveled as far as thirty miles for the festivities. Guns were checked at the door, and if there was any drinking, it was done in the barn. Sleepy children were laid crosswise on the beds, tucked in like little sardines in a can. Their lullaby was a soulful sonata or sprightly jig played on Herb Bassett's violin. John Jarvie, a Scotsman who was one of the Park's first settlers, played the accordion and organ and could render over one hundred tunes by ear. Butch Cassidy never missed a dance and often accompanied the organ player with his harmonica, while Harry Longabaugh (the Sundance Kid) played popular tunes on his clarinet. When it was a neighbor's turn to host a party, the Bassetts loaded their organ into a wagon and took it along. That organ arrived at parties by wagon, buckboard, and even in a buggy.

Everyone came to the dances, which lasted till dawn as guests spun and twirled to waltzes, polkas, jigs, and reels. Since there were no large halls or ballrooms available, they cleared out all the furniture and rugs from the main room or kitchen, making space for dancing. When the sun came up, they shared a huge breakfast before they wearily headed home.

Besides being a place for parties, the Bassett home was a comfortable place to relax and read a book. Herb Bassett had a wonderful library of the classics, volumes of poetry, the complete works of Shakespeare, and the writings of Keats, Shelly, Longfellow, Dickens, and Byron that he'd brought from Arkansas. Butch Cassidy was often found there, boots off, feet up, enjoying his favorite Dickens novel or a volume of world history.

In 1892, Elizabeth Bassett died suddenly after an attack of severe abdominal pain, possibly due to a ruptured appendix or a miscarriage. The December 16, 1892 issue of *Empire Courier* praised her as "a natural pioneer possessing the most remarkable courage and energy." After Elizabeth's death, Josie and Ann took up the battle against the powerful Wyoming stockmen. Although both sisters were involved, Ann was better known and was dubbed "Queen Ann" and "Queen of the Rustlers."

The wealthy cattlemen pressured the sisters to sell the ranch and hired cowboys to harass them and stampede their cattle. The Bassetts turned to the outlaws for help, and Kid Curry, who'd killed several men, warned the hired cowboys to leave the sisters alone "or else." His threats were effective and eased the pressure on the Bassett women. In November 1895, the outlaws decided to show their appreciation to the families of Brown's Park for their generosity and tolerance. Butch Cassidy, Elza Lay, Isom Dart, the Sundance Kid, Billie Bender, and Les Megs planned a festive holiday feast, known as the "outlaws' Thanksgiving dinner."

The ladies planned their outfits for weeks, and Ann Bassett described everyone's finery in detail. Black taffeta was the choice for the older women's long, fitted dresses with leg of mutton sleeves and high collars. The younger ladies wore elegant, brightly colored gowns. The men dressed in dark suits, white shirts with starched collars and bowties. Their mustaches were waxed and curled, and their beards were neatly trimmed.

The dinner party was held at the Davenport ranch, and the fine china, silver, and linens were provided by the ladies of Brown's Park. Elizabeth Bassett's silver candelabra added an elegant touch to the long dinner table. Isom Dart presided over the kitchen, wearing a tall white chef's hat and an apron. He baked, chopped, and stewed with the help of the boys for days to prepare the sumptuous feast.

The dinner party lasted about six hours, and when they couldn't eat another bite, everyone headed for the dance floor. There was plenty of music, and the guests twirled and waltzed until the sun came up the next morning. Then they piled in their wagons and buggies and headed home, pronouncing it the best party ever held in Brown's Park.

In late 1899, Hi Bernard, the manager of the Two Bar Ranch, and ranch owner Ora Haley met John Coble and two other wealthy Wyoming ranchers in Haley's Denver office. They agreed to hire Tom Horn, a Pinkerton detective, to rid the range of rustlers who hung out in Brown's Park. Horn would be paid $500 for every cattle thief he killed, and Matt Rash and Jim McKnight were to be eliminated soon.

Tom Horn, using the name "Tom Hicks," rode into Brown's Park in early 1900, posing as a cowboy and horse buyer. Ann Bassett, who was engaged to Rash, was immediately suspicious, and Josie insisted, "Something's not right with him." Horn worked briefly for Rash as a cook and wrangler and moved around Brown's Park, spying and gathering information. First, he focused on Jim McKnight, whose marriage to Josie was in trouble. She'd started divorce proceedings, and when a deputy tried to serve the legal papers, Jim angrily threw them on the ground. As he walked away, the deputy shot him. Jim was seriously wounded, so Tom Hicks (Horn) rode forty-seven miles to Vernal, Utah, for the doctor. He sent a telegram to McKnight's family in Salt Lake City, informing them of the shooting.

The doctor returned with Hicks and treated Jim's wound. Jim's brother came from Utah and cared for him during his recovery. The divorce papers were signed, and when he was well enough, Jim McKnight left Brown's Park. This incident probably saved his life, because his name was at the top of Horn's list. Matt Rash received a threatening letter that told him to sell out and leave the county within thirty days or be killed. After discussing this with Ann and his friends, Rash decided he would not be driven out of Brown's Park. He spent the Fourth of July in Rock Springs, and on his way home, he stopped at the Bassett ranch to see Ann.

On July 10, 1900, the decomposing body of Matt Rash was found in his cabin by two boys. A coroner's jury was summoned and conducted an inquest on the spot. It was determined that Rash was sitting at his table when he was shot in the back and then the chest by the killer. After the inquest, Rash was buried next to his cabin. Rash's father and brother came from Texas to handle his affairs and take his body home. During these arrangements, Tom Hicks showed up and claimed that he and Rash had been close friends. He tried to cast suspicion on Isom Dart, saying he'd seen the two men arguing. This created suspicions of Hicks, because everyone knew Rash and Isom Dart had been friends for years. Matt Rash's body was exhumed, returned to Texas, and buried in his family's plot. Ann was heartbroken by the loss of her fiancé and believed Tom Hicks was the murderer. She went to the sheriff with her suspicions, but the lawman did nothing.

After Elizabeth Bassett's death, Isom Dart, who was about forty-two years old, spent more time at Josie and Jim McKnight's place on Cold Spring Mountain. He helped clear the land and build a large log cabin and corrals.

He cooked, handled household tasks, lent a hand with Josie's youngsters, and continued to break and train horses. The two McKnight boys enjoyed sitting around a huge bonfire with Dart as he played the fiddle and harmonica and taught them songs of the Old South.

Dart became partners with John Dempshire in the ownership of his horses and herd of cattle. When Josie and the boys relocated to Craig after the divorce, Dart moved into the McKnight cabin and took care of Josie's cattle. Sam and George Bassett and two cowboys came by to visit on October 2, 1900, and spent the night. The next morning, as Dart was walking to the corral, two shots rang out, and he fell, dead. The others stayed inside the cabin until they thought the shooter was gone, and then they came out and discovered Dart's body. They hurriedly saddled up and rode down the mountain to report another murder.

Josie McKnight and several other well-armed citizens hurried to the ranch and found Dart's body. The justice of the peace impaneled a jury, and the inquest was held promptly. Dart had been shot twice, and two empty .30-.30 shells had been found near the corral. The killer had tied his horse to a grove of aspens as he waited for Dart, and Sam Bassett followed the horse's hoofprints for several miles before they disappeared.

It was snowing lightly when they buried Isom Dart in the aspen grove west of the cabin. Many of the mourners had known him since they were children. Josie said sadly, "He was just a good, honest, old colored man who never hurt anybody." Years later, Joe Davenport was interviewed about Isom Dart for the April 4, 1929 issue of the *Rock Springs Rocket.* He said, "Of Isom Dart, Negro cow puncher of the early days, old-timers speak reverently. He was in a way the Gunga Din of Brown's Park during the '80s, and his engaging personality was such that he left an ineffable imprint in many minds, both for his daring deeds and his unswerving integrity." Davenport continued, "I worked side by side with him for years, and he taught me all the tricks of riding. Isom was the most polite man I ever met and was a courtier supreme in his respect for women. I have seen all the great riders. But for all-around skill as a cowman, Isom Dart was unexcelled, and I never saw his peer." Davenport concluded, "He kept his place and invariably ate his meals in silence alone, although not a cowman ever objected to his company."

Ann Bassett was devastated by the deaths of Matt Rash and Isom Dart and believed Ora Haley was responsible for the murders. She asked everyone for help patrolling the park's rangeland, but many were too frightened. In late November 1900, she received a warning letter: "You are requested to leave the country for parts unknown within thirty days or you will be killed—thirty days for your life." It was signed, "Committee."

Elbert Bassett received a similar letter, and both were postmarked from Cheyenne. Ann's letter was printed in the December 8 edition of the *Craig Courier.* Despite the public clamor for action, Routt County Sheriff Farnham didn't go near Brown's Park, and there wasn't any investigation of the murders. The newspapers became involved, and there was a series of headlines that made the wealthy cattlemen uncomfortable. The December 20, 1900 *Denver Post* screamed, "War on a Woman" and "Wyoming in It," while the headline "Cattlemen May be Murderers" in the *Wyoming Tribune* worried Horn's employers. The *Craig Courier* observed that the sheriff's inaction meant that the assassinations in Brown's Park would likely continue.

One dark night in January 1901, Ann was sitting at the living room table when two bullets blasted through the door, narrowly missing her head. There'd been no alarm because the shooter had killed their watch dog. This attack scared Ann, but it did not stop her battle against Haley. For the next two years, she and her brother Eb ran the ranch while young George and Sam were in school in Missouri. Herb was much older now but still handled the business finances, and Ann continued to fight the Two Bar.

Ann and everyone in Brown's Park were relieved when Tom Horn was hanged in November 1903 for killing fourteen-year-old Willie Nickell in Wyoming. In 1904, Ann ended her romantic relationship with Butch Cassidy and never saw him again after he left for South America. In April, Ann surprised everyone by marrying Hi Bernard, Ora Haley's ranch manager, who was immediately fired. Ann, her brothers, and Bernard formed a partnership to develop their cattle enterprise.

In 1911, Ann was arrested for rustling Two Bar cattle, and the shocking news filled the newspapers. The March 29, 1911 *Cheyenne State Leader* headline "Queen Ann Is Behind Bars for Rustling" sold a lot of papers; while another banner in the April 1, 1911 *Craig Empire Courier* screamed "Famed Cattle Queen Hauled into Court." The courtroom was packed, but the trial ended in a hung jury. There was a second trial in August 1913 in Craig. Once again, spectators crowded the courtroom in support of Ann, who'd fought the wealthy cattlemen for years. The jury deliberated for eight hours and returned the verdict, "Not guilty!" The *Craig Courier* of August 16, 1913, trumpeted, "Businesses Close. Bands Blare. Town of Craig Goes Wild with Joy!" An August 16 article in the *Denver Republican* summarized the whoops and gunshots that marked the celebration as a brass band led the parade. Queen Ann was driven around Craig in an automobile before she invited everyone to the free movie at the theater. Then the celebration hit Main Street, where the band played lively tunes, and everyone danced the night away.

In 1913, Ann and Hi Bernard divorced, and in 1917, Ora Haley sold the Two Bar. He died in 1919. In 1928, Ann married Frank Willis, an engineer, and they ran a small ranch in Utah. Ann died on May 8, 1986, a few days before her seventy-ninth birthday.

Author's Note: The BLM (Bureau of Land Management) maintains the historic Jarvie Ranch, which has been designated the Brown's Park National Wildlife Refuge.

10

TOM HORN

BOUNTY HUNTER

Tom Horn bragged to U.S. Marshal Joe LeFors on January 12, 1902, "Killing men is my specialty. I look at it as a business proposition, and I think I have a corner on the market." The two men were talking about the murder of Willie Nickell, a fourteen-year-old boy, and Horn was the main suspect.

LeFors knew Horn often boasted about killings that he'd done and decided to set a trap. Tom Horn stepped right into it without thinking. He foolishly volunteered information and answered the marshal's questions about the Nickell murder with no hesitation, incriminating himself. Horn didn't know a deputy was listening in an adjacent room and that a stenographer was writing down every word he said. The following morning, after a judge reviewed a transcript of the conversation, he issued a bench warrant for Horn's arrest. Less than twenty-four hours after bragging, "I shot the kid at three hundred yards," Horn landed in jail. He commented, "It was the best shot and dirtiest trick I ever done." How did this experienced range detective and former Pinkerton agent reach this low point in his life?

Tom Horn was born in Missouri in 1860, a few months before the first shots of the Civil War were fired. The fifth of twelve children born to his hardworking parents, Tom avoided church and the classroom, preferring instead to hunt with his dog. After being severely punished after another day in the woods, he left home at fourteen and found work with the railroad, laying tracks in Kansas. He joined a cattle drive from Texas to Dodge City and then headed to Colorado. After working in the Leadville silver mines, he drifted south and drove Overland Mail stages across the Arizona Territory.

In Arizona, several thousand Apaches had been driven from their homeland and confined to the barren San Carlos Reservation. Led by Geronimo, or Victorio, the Apaches often fled their reservation to plunder and kill their way to Mexico. In 1882, Horn was hired by the army as a civilian and worked at a variety of jobs. He was proficient in Spanish and was learning the Apache language when he joined Al Sieber and his Apache scouts. They pursued renegade Apaches into Mexico in 1883 and 1885, and Horn was with General Miles's expedition when Geronimo surrendered in 1886.

With the end of Apache hostilities, Horn left the army and prospected for silver with Al Sieber, but in 1887, he became involved in the Pleasant Valley War, a bloody feud between the Graham and Tewskbury factions. Horn was a Tewksbury supporter, and in 1888, when a friend, Glenn Reynolds, was elected sheriff of Gila County, Horn became his deputy. He competed in local rodeos and won the "World Champion Calf Roping" contest. He eventually pulled up stakes and headed north to Prescott. He served briefly as Sheriff Bucky O'Neil's deputy but left to join the unsuccessful manhunt for the Apache Kid.

In 1890, Horn assisted Doc Shores, the sheriff of Gunnison County, Colorado, capture a gang of horse thieves who'd escaped to Arizona. Doc recommended Horn to the Pinkerton Agency, and he was hired. Horn quickly became bored with that job, and in 1892, he headed for Wyoming, where he became a stock detective for the Stock Growers Association. Horn offered no details about his employment, and in his autobiography, *Life of Tom Horn*, he simply wrote "1892 came to Wyoming."

Large cattle companies competed with small ranchers and homesteaders for Wyoming range land. Wealthy ranchers seized control of much of the open public domain land that could be used for raising cattle or homesteading. The Stock Growers Association controlled many state agencies and influenced land policies, but homesteaders began claiming more public domain land, reducing cattlemen's free grazing land. Large numbers of cattle died in the unusually harsh winter of 1886–87, as they starved on over-grazed land where there wasn't enough forage.

The stockmen claimed homesteaders were stealing their cattle, and they were determined to drive them out or hang them. They seized control of homesteaders' water sources and wouldn't allow small ranchers to take part in the annual spring roundup. This prevented them from retrieving their own cattle from public lands. They made it difficult for small ranchers to register their new brands, and then they hired stock inspectors to confiscate their animals at shipping points.

As more homesteaders, ranchers, and small businessmen settled in Wyoming, they served on juries and held elections. The newly elected judges often dismissed charges against homesteaders and delayed or postponed their trials. Stockmen claimed it was difficult to get a guilty verdict against cattle thieves and insisted this justified lynching them. In 1886, Thomas Sturgis, secretary of the Stock Growers Association, said, "It is almost completely useless to bring cattle stealing matters to court even after an indictment has been obtained....There seems to be a morbid sympathy with cattle thieves both on the bench and in the jury room."

The Stock Growers Association hired more stock detectives to catch rustlers. These detectives were believed to be responsible for the deaths of several small ranchers who were suspected of rustling. The lynching of Ella Watson (Cattle Kate) and Jim Averell for rustling enraged homesteaders and small ranchers, who started their own organization, the Northern Wyoming Farmers and Stock Growers Association.

In 1892, tensions between the stockmen and the small ranchers and homesteaders escalated into the Johnson County War. A large group of wealthy stockmen and hired gunmen from Texas to invade the area around Buffalo with the intention of lynching or shooting seventy men whose names they carried on a list. Several were killed, and a posse of four hundred homesteaders closed in on the invaders, who holed up at the T.A. Ranch. Their plan to dynamite the ranch was disrupted by the arrival of the Sixth Cavalry and a unit of Buffalo Soldiers. The troops escorted the invading gunmen to Fort Russell, near Cheyenne for trial. Before this could happen, they were all released on bail. Many fled to Texas and were never seen again. The charges against these invaders were eventually dropped, infuriating the public. Newspapers accused the Pinkerton Agency and Tom Horn of being involved, but there was no evidence to prove that charge.

Tom Horn began breaking horses for the Swan Land and Cattle Company and remained on the alert for rustlers on the ranch's six hundred thousand acres. He became disgusted with the legal system after a gang of rustlers he'd caught went free or received light sentences. He decided there was no use going to the expense of a trial when a conviction was impossible. In 1895, he met briefly with Governor Richards, a strong supporter of the cattlemen and the owner of a ranch in the Big Horn Valley. Richards was losing cattle to rustlers, and Horn alluded to the way he'd solve this problem but didn't offer specifics. He concluded by saying, "I have a system that never fails."

Horn met with leaders of the cattle industry at the Cheyenne Club and proposed that he'd do what was necessary to rid the country of rustlers. He

Left: Tom Horn in his younger years. *Public domain.*

Right: WSGA range detective badge. *American Heritage Center, University of Wyoming.*

reminded them, "I have a system that never fails. Yours has." The cattlemen tacitly agreed that there was nothing to prevent a cattle company or an individual from contracting with Horn to "inflict the maximum penalty on beef-stealing thieves." They were determined to stop rustling and to run the homesteaders out by any means. Since their previous plan had failed in Johnson County, a few men decided to support Horn's proposal of "selective assassination."

It didn't take long for word to get around that Tom Horn was willing to get rid of rustlers permanently for $500 a head. Within six weeks in 1895, two suspected rustlers, William Lewis and Fred Powell, were murdered. Lewis was an unsavory character who'd spent time in jail for stealing clothes. Then he moved up to stealing cattle. He was tried for rustling and was found guilty but requested a new jury trial, and their verdict was "not guilty."

Lewis was arrested again for stealing cattle from Horn's employer, the Swan Land and Cattle Company, and once again, the jury found him not guilty. Then Lewis sued the company executives who'd had him arrested and demanded $15,000 because they had damaged him financially. Lewis received death threats, was shot at twice, and finally, his house was burned down. He moved but continued to receive notes that told him to leave the area or face the consequences. He'd won his previous court cases, and with the growing hostility toward the cattle barons, there was a good possibility that he'd win again.

On July 31, 1895, as Lewis was loading a beef carcass into a wagon, he was shot three times and died on the spot. His decomposing body wasn't found until August 3. He was buried nearby, and a coroner's inquest was held. There was a grand jury investigation, and a dozen witnesses were called, including Tom Horn. He testified that he'd been out of the area with the manager of the Swan Company at the time of Lewis's murder. This murder case was never solved.

Fred Powell had lost his arm in an accident while he was working for the railroad. He was transferred to another job but was eventually fired after he robbed a passenger. He was good with a horse and lasso and started ranching but had trouble with his neighbors. They said he stole from them, tore down fences, and started fires, so they went to the sheriff. Powell was hauled into court several times to face charges of larceny, malicious trespassing, theft, and rustling, but he was usually released on bond.

In July 1895, Powell stole a horse but was caught, arrested, tried, and found guilty. He appealed and was released on bond. Next, he served four months in jail for arson. When he was released, he received threatening letters that told him to leave the county or be killed.

On September 10, 1895, Andy Ross, a handyman, and Powell were repairing a fence. Ross went for more wood, heard a single shot and returned to find Powell's body. He fled to a neighboring ranch, where he told the mail carrier about the murder, and she notified the sheriff in Laramie. No one was ever arrested for this killing.

There were two sides to Horn's personality. Sober, he was usually quiet, taciturn, and did not socialize or mix with others. He was distant with women and tried to avoid them. He liked children; he gave them candy and often allowed them to ride his horse. After some drinks, he became loud, overbearing, and boastful. "I'm the best shot in the United States!" he bragged. He went on benders that lasted seven to fourteen days.

In 1898, a reporter interviewed Horn as he headed for the Spanish American War. This gave him the opportunity to spin exaggerated tales of his exploits in the West. He claimed he'd been fighting Natives Americans for eighteen years to avenge his father, an army scout, who'd had been killed by the Apaches. (His father was a Missouri farmer and never served in the army.) He bragged that he'd commanded one hundred Apache scouts and personally arranged a peace treaty with the renegades.

His autobiography was exaggerated, and in it, he announced that he was a colonel in the Spanish American War who supervised all the pack trains in Cuba. Horn was really a civilian army employee who served as the pack master of Pack Train no. 3, and he took orders from a lieutenant. Before the war ended, he was promoted to the position of chief packer of the pack trains in William Shafter's Fifth U.S. Army Corps. He hauled supplies to the Buffalo Soldiers and Teddy Roosevelt's Rough Riders and came home with yellow fever. He spent the winter of 1898–99 recuperating at John Coble's Iron Mountain Ranch.

Tom Horn worked off and on for the Pinkertons and was a Union Pacific Railroad detective when the Wild Bunch held up a train at Wilcox, Wyoming, on June 2, 1899. They stole $50,000, split the money, and disappeared. The reward of $3,000 per outlaw, dead or alive, offered by the railroad motivated Horn and Ed Tewksbury of Arizona. They killed two men near Jackson Hole and left the bodies where they fell. Tom applied for the reward, boasting that they'd killed these two members of the Cassidy Gang who'd robbed the Wilcox train. He got his stories mixed up, and newspapers pointed this out. When the two dead men were identified, it was learned that neither one had been involved in the Wilcox train robbery.

As if that uproar wasn't bad enough, Horn was responsible for killing two men in Wyoming's Red Desert. Once again, he filed for the Wilcox robbery reward, claiming that these men were part of the gang that held up the train. When railroad officials insisted on seeing the bodies of the two men, Horn finally took them near the spot where he'd shot them. The corpses were dug up—but these men weren't the train robbers either. Horn insisted he'd shot these two victims because they were outlaws who'd pulled their guns on him. However, it was quickly discovered that neither man had a weapon. When this latest story appeared in the newspapers, the dead men's names were published, identifying them as two well-known prospectors. When Horn joked that these four killings were "apparently a funny mistake," the public was infuriated. The February 10, 1900 *Carbon County Journal* wrote, "This shows a reckless disregard for human life." The publication wondered whether lawmen were going to follow a policy of "shoot first—identify later."

The public's suspicions about Tom Horn grew, and as more newspapers scrutinized his man-hunting activities, there were more questions. It looked like the railroad employed rogue detectives, who were motivated to kill just to collect the cash reward. When he was drinking, Horn's boasts about the outlaws he'd killed became louder and more detailed, leading to more questions about his involvement in the murders of homesteaders Lewis and Powell.

Ora Haley, a friend of John Coble, owned the Two Bar Ranch, one of the largest in Wyoming. At the time, Haley was pushing his cattle into Brown's

Park in northwestern Colorado. Surrounded by mountains, Brown's Park's grasslands were bisected by the Green River, making it ideal for livestock. The valley was coveted by Haley, who needed more land for his huge herds. As Haley's cattle grazed on pastureland that the established Brown's Park homesteaders considered theirs, they didn't hesitate to butcher a Haley steer or slap their brand on an unmarked calf.

In early 1900, wealthy cattlemen John Coble, Willard Wilson, and Charley Ayer met with Hi Bernard, the Two Bar Ranch manager. They agreed to hire someone to rid the range of rustlers and eliminate the opposition of homesteaders and ranchers in Brown's Park. They agreed to pay $500 for every rustler that was killed. Ayer collected half the money from Haley and the other half came from Wilson and Ayer. Haley told Hi Bernard to provide supplies and horses to Horn, who took the job and resigned from the Union Pacific.

Tom Horn rode into Brown's Park in April 1890 and was hired as a cook at Matt Rash's small ranch. He said his name was Tom Hicks, and he claimed he wasn't much of a cowboy. Ann Bassett, who was engaged to Rash, was suspicious of Hicks immediately. She said, "His bragging that he'd been a great Indian fighter—his boastful descriptive accounts of the human slaughter he'd accomplished single-handed were exceedingly obnoxious."

Hicks tried to ingratiate himself with the Brown's Park ranchers, but some saw through his act and avoided him. When Josie Bassett's husband, Jim McKnight, was accidentally shot and seriously wounded, the nearest doctor was forty-five miles away in Vernal, Utah. Tom Hicks made the ride and brought the doctor back for the man who was at the top of his suspect list.

Tom Hicks eavesdropped, spied, and moved around stealthily, making a list of Brown's Park residents he believed were stealing cattle from Haley and other stockmen. Hi Bernard, the Two Bar manager, related later that they met with Hicks, and he presented his "evidence" that Brown's Park homesteaders were rustling. Horn was given the "go ahead signal" to kill the guilty ones, and payment was guaranteed.

Horn worked briefly for Matt Rash where his mysterious comings and goings aroused suspicions. On May 6, 1900, George Banks overheard Hicks, Hi Bernard, and a man called Mexican Pete talking in a Craig livery stable. They discussed plans to murder Matt Rash, Isom Dart, and several others whom Hicks suspected of rustling. Ann Bassett, her brother Elbert, and rancher Joe Davenport would receive warning letters. Banks acted as if he hadn't overheard this conversation, but a few days later, someone fired several shots at him.

By June 1890, Hicks was leaving unsigned letters on the doors of suspects, ordering them to "leave Brown's Park within 30 days or suffer the consequences." Matt Rash received a threatening letter, but decided he was not going to leave Brown's Park. On July 7, he returned from Rock Springs, Wyoming, and stopped to see Ann Bassett. Three days later, on July 10, his body was found in his cabin by two boys. His horse was lying by the door, a bullet through its head. A coroner's jury was summoned immediately, and the inquest was conducted on the spot. They concluded that Rash had been shot as he sat at the table eating, but he managed to crawl to his bunk, where he died. He was buried behind his cabin.

Tom Hicks (Horn) immediately headed for Baggs, Wyoming, where he walked into the Bulldog Saloon about 3:00 a.m.; he was soon drunk and bragging loudly. He started a fight with the two Kelly brothers, and one pulled a knife and slashed him on the neck. The wound was deep and bled profusely. Horn collapsed, but bystanders quickly moved him to the hotel, where a doctor stopped the bleeding and sutured the wound. Word went around that the Kelly brothers were going to "finish him off, "so a deputy stayed with Horn for days until he was able to ride out of Baggs."

Many people suspected that Tom Horn had killed Matt Rash, and Ann Bassett wasn't afraid to voice her opinions. In September 1890, Horn returned to Brown's Park and didn't try to hide his real identity. Using his own name, he signed a complaint accusing Isom Dart of stealing horses. Dart was frightened and holed up in his cabin on Cold Spring Mountain with some friends. On the cold, windy morning of October 4, 1900, Dart stepped out of his front door and headed for the corral. Two shots rang out, and he fell dead. The others who were with him stayed in the cabin until they were sure the killer was gone. They found two .30-.30 shells at the base of the pine tree near the corral where the killer had hidden. After the inquest at his cabin, Dart was buried nearby.

These murders persuaded some of Horn's suspects to quickly leave Brown's Park. Ed Bassett and Joe Davenport received warning letters that gave them sixty days to clear out. Elijah "Longhorn" Thompson narrowly escaped Horn's bullets and fled to Utah. He later said that he was the only man Tom Horn ever missed. Joe Davenport departed for Missouri and recalled that everyone in the park was certain they were going to be Horn's next victim. The Bassets received another threatening letter, and someone shot at Ann through a window one night, narrowly missing her.

In November 1900, Horn was interviewed by the *Wyoming Tribune*, and if there had been any doubt about his role in Brown's Park, the mouthy detective's boastfulness dismissed it. He didn't admit to killing Rash or Dart, but he assured the reporter that "two more notorious rustlers would never infest the Rocky Mountain country." He announced that Brown's Park "had been freed of undesirable elements so respectable stockmen could settle there."

Several newspapers wagered that wealthy Wyoming stockmen had employed an assassin in Brown's Park and speculated about Horn's part in the murders. The December 5, 1900 *Steamboat Pilot* presented the explosive theory that the governors of Colorado, Wyoming, and Utah had met to discuss using violence to "clean out the highwaymen and rustlers in the three corners area." The *Pilot* asserted that a Wyoming stock detective had been hired and concluded "what his instructions were none, may know, but his deadly work speaks for itself." The December 22, 1900 *Rocky Mountain News* and the December 23 *Wyoming Tribune* repeated these accusations.

The cattlemen were slow to pay Horn $500 for killing Isom Dart, asserting that Jim McBride was their intended target. Writer Charles Kelly said Horn "was refused payment until he became nasty and demanded payment "or else." Horn was drinking more now, and his alcoholic benders became more frequent. After a few drinks, he lost all sense of caution and talked too much, foolishly bragging about killing seventeen men. He dropped enough hints that listeners could figure out the victims' identities. Bud Cowan, a cowboy who broke horses with him, said, "As a friend, Tom was true blue, and as an enemy, he was deadly." He always carried a forty-foot-long rawhide rope and was very good with the lasso. He had learned to braid ropes using horsehair or leather from the Apaches and was an accomplished braider of hackamores, ropes, and lariats.

In 1885, Kels Nickell was homesteading near John Coble's huge Iron Mountain Ranch. He had a fiery temper, was generally disagreeable, and managed to offend all his neighbors. He got into a loud argument with John Coble, pulled out his knife and slashed the rancher's abdomen, inflicting a terrible wound. The rancher, a close friend of Tom Horn, hovered near death for days, but he finally began to recover. During Coble's long convalescence, his anger at Nickell smoldered and grew.

Kels Nickell had an ongoing feud with Jim Miller, another homesteader who lived about a mile away. Nickell began raising sheep and brought in one thousand animals that often invaded Miller's fields. The two had taken shots at each other, and each man kept a loaded gun close at hand. This led to a tragic accident in which Miller's shotgun accidentally discharged and hit his son in the head, killing him, and seriously injuring his daughter.

A photograph of Willie Nickell taken shortly before his murder. *American Heritage Center, University of Wyoming.*

When the two enemies met accidentally in a restaurant, Nickell stabbed Miller in the shoulder.

On July 18, 1901, fourteen-year-old Willie Nickell left the house early in the morning, riding his father's horse. He was gone all day, and when he didn't return that night, his family wasn't worried, as they thought he'd stayed overnight at neighbor's ranch. The next morning, his brother Frank found Willie's body about a mile from home, lying in the road. He'd been shot three times, and his shirt was ripped open to expose his wounds. Frank raced home, and Kels sent for the sheriff in Cheyenne. The coroner's inquest began at the Nickell home and continued off and on for several months.

On August 4, 1901, an unknown gunman shot Kels Nickell as he was milking cows in a pasture. He had serious wounds, but his life was saved by a quick trip to the hospital. Later, masked riders attacked his flock of sheep and killed thirty-five animals after they chased off the shepherd.

In early August, Deputy U.S. Marshal Joe LeFors joined the investigation into the murder of Willie Nickell. LeFors spent weeks perfecting a plan in which Horn's boasts would lead him into a compromising conversation that would disclose his part in the killing of young Willie Nickell. LeFors arranged for a friend to write a letter to him about an available stock detective position in Montana. Then he made sure Horn learned about this letter and the job from John Coble, whom he trusted. More letters were exchanged, and Horn, who wanted this position badly, assured the Montana stockholders of their "satisfaction." A fake job offer was made to Horn, and he sent a letter to LeFors saying he would like to visit with him and pick up a railroad pass for a trip to Montana. Horn wanted to meet LeFors around January 10, when he returned from taking horses to Omaha. LeFors set his trap.

LeFors and Horn met in the marshal's office in Cheyenne. Horn had already visited several saloons and was anxious to talk about the Montana stock detective job. LeFors had stationed Deputy Leslie Snow and stenographer Charlie Ohnhaus in the adjacent room, near a slightly open door. The deputy was to witness this meeting and the conversation, which was to be recorded in shorthand and transcribed by Ohnhaus.

The liquor relaxed Horn, and he and LeFors, a former stock detective himself, shared a few stories. Horn said he killed his first man when he was twenty-six years old. The marshal eased into a conversation about the recent murders and casually asked if he had any trouble collecting money for a killing. Horn replied, "A man would have to pay for a job like that."

Joe LeFors, deputy U.S. marshal, 1898. *American Heritage Center, University of Wyoming.*

LeFors commented, "You got paid $600 apiece for killing Lewis and Powell, didn't you? You were paid $300 for the Nickell job. Why did you cut the price?" Horn sliced off a piece of chewing tobacco, slouched down in his chair, and replied, "I got $2,100 for killing three men." Then he said cooly, "Killing men is my specialty."

As they talked, the marshal occasionally slipped in a question about the murder of Willie Nickell. When he asked, "How far was Willie Nickell killed?" Horn casually replied, "About three hundred yards" Then he boasted, "It was the best shot that I ever made and the dirtiest trick that I ever done." He said he picked up the cartridge shells after he shot the boy. Horn's careless answers were incriminating, but LeFors said nothing and invited him for a drink in a nearby saloon. Later, they returned to LeFors's office and continued their conversation.

Tom Horn braiding a rope in the Laramie County Jail's office in Cheyenne, 1902. *American Heritage Center, University of Wyoming.*

Historians vary on the number of saloon visits the pair made. Horn had been drinking before he met LeFors, but it's surprising that he talked so freely, since he'd been warned that he was in danger. Perhaps he was so arrogant that he thought he could escape any reprisal—or maybe he thought his cattlemen friends would handle the problems as they always had. Horn eventually left the marshal's office, expecting to head to Montana the following day. That night the stenographer, Ohnhaus, typed his shorthand notes, and in the morning, the document was reviewed by the judge. The judge issued a bench warrant for Horn's arrest, and the sheriff was given the job of bringing him in. On January 13, 1902, Tom Horn was arrested at the Cheyenne Inter-Ocean Hotel and taken to jail. The news of his arrest caused a stir in Wyoming and Colorado. On January 24, at a preliminary hearing, the judge ruled there was sufficient evidence to hold him in jail without bail.

Horn's trial began on Friday October 10 and lasted until October 24, 1902. It drew newspapermen from as far away as New York, and the papers followed the proceedings closely. A blue-ribbon team of lawyers, led by former Judge John Lacey of Indiana, was assembled for Horn's defense. The prosperous Wyoming cattlemen paid his legal expenses but tried to distance themselves from him. The man who was once an asset had become a serious liability. They did not want to be associated with any murder-for-hire scheme, and none of the cattlemen took the stand on Horn's behalf.

Tom Horn's grave, Columbia Cemetery, Boulder, Colorado. *Photograph by Tom Williams.*

The district attorney presented the evidence, including the record of Horn's incriminating conversation with Deputy Marshal LeFors. The defense challenged this, but the record was accepted. The case went to the jury, which reached a decision in about five hours. Horn was returned to the courtroom to hear the clerk read the verdict: guilty of first-degree murder. The verdict surprised some, but it was obvious that Horn had been his own worst enemy.

The case was appealed, and the request for a new trial was denied. The execution date of November 20, 1903, was set. Horn passed his time in jail braiding hackamores and lassos and writing his autobiography, The *Life of Tom Horn, Government Scout and Interpreter, Written by Himself.* His story filled four notebooks, which he gave to John Coble to be published.

Tom Horn was hanged in Cheyenne on November 20, 1903, one day before his forty-fourth birthday. Charles Horn took his brother's body, valise, and unfinished horsehair braiding to Boulder, Colorado. A large crowd attended Horn's funeral, and he was buried in Columbia Cemetery in Boulder. John Coble paid for Horn's coffin and the granite monument on his grave.

11

TOM McCARTY

TEACHER OF OUTLAWS

Tom McCarty was the mastermind who planned each bank robbery and train holdup he committed and devised how he'd take every horse or calf he stole. He spent days studying his target, its location, schedules, and employees' routines. He planned his escape route carefully and used the best horses he could buy or steal, conditioning them for speed and endurance. Relay animals were located strategically along his escape route. He made sure that everyone involved knew what his job was. McCarty's careful planning and preparation paid off, and the gang successfully rustled plenty of cattle, stole many horses, and committed a string of train and bank robberies without mishap—until September 7, 1893, when everything went wrong.

The day dawned warm and breezy in Delta, Colorado, as Tom McCarty, his brother Bill, and his eighteen-year-old son, Fred, left Bailey's Saloon across Main Street from the Farmers and Merchants Bank. They mounted their horses and rode to the alley behind the bank, where Fred and Bill dismounted and handed the reins to Tom. The pair walked around the bank building and went inside. There were no customers, and the cashier, Trew Blachly, and his assistant, Harry Wolbert, had just opened the safe and put out cash for the day's business. They looked up and saw two six-shooters pointed at them as Bill ordered, "Hands up! This is a holdup!" Fred jumped over a partition and was standing on the counter when Blachly suddenly yelled and lunged for the gun that was lying on his desk. Fred fired, but his first shot missed and plowed straight into the floor. The second bullet struck

Main Street Delta, 1897. *Denver Public Library Special Collections.*

Blachly's head, killing him instantly. The robbers hurriedly scooped up the currency on the counter, shoved it into their pockets, and rushed out the bank's back door.

In the alley, Tom McCarty was holding his gun on an attorney named Robertson who'd come out of his office at the rear of the building. When Tom heard the shots, he knew something was wrong inside, and he quickly tied the horses to a post. Then he started up the alley just as Bill and Fred rushed out and jumped on their mounts. Fred McCarty dropped a bag of gold coins as he and Bill raced after Tom.

The shots had drawn a small crowd to the front of the bank, while in the hardware store across the street, Ray Simpson grabbed his rifle and a handful of bullets. He ran toward the alley and heard the clatter of hooves as Tom burst out, followed by Fred and Bill. Simpson took aim, squeezed the trigger, and hit Bill in the back of his head. The robber tumbled out of his saddle, and Simpson ran to the body and reloaded as Fred looked back toward his father. Simpson fired again and hit Fred in the head, knocking him from his horse. Then he took aim and shot at Tom, who was racing toward the bridge across the Gunnison River. His shots fell short, as Tom was out of range. It didn't take Tom long to realize that Bill and Fred were not galloping behind him.

The sheriff quickly assembled a six-man posse, and they rode out of Delta, following Tom McCarty's trail. As darkness came on, they lost his tracks in the rugged canyons between Delta and Grand Junction, so they turned back. The bodies of the robbers were taken to the furniture store, where the owner was an undertaker who made coffins as well as furniture. A large portion of Bill's head had been blown away by Simpson's bullet, so a hat was used to cover the damage. Bill and Fred were propped up against a wall, and photographs were taken. Neither was identified, as they had nothing in their pockets except some bullets and a few bills.

The day after the robbery, a $500 reward was offered for the capture, dead or alive, of the outlaw who'd escaped. The newspaper published the description of the man: he was about five feet, seven inches tall; weighed about 150 pounds; had dark hair and a dark beard; and was wearing a gray coat over overalls. Bill and Fred were buried in a single coffin in potters' field at the Delta Cemetery. Over the next two days, they were disinterred several times for lawmen who came to take a look at and possibly identify them.

Farmers and Merchants Bank, Delta, Colorado. *Delta County Historical Society.*

Bill and Fred McCarty, dead. *Delta County Historical Society*.

Fred was recognized quickly, but for some reason, everyone claimed Bill was Tom McCarty. It was a while before Bill was correctly identified.

Apparently, Tom remained in the Delta area until he learned what really happened to his brother and nephew. A second posse, led by former Sheriff Gheen, found his camp, and on September 11, they came upon a fresh trail. They followed it south for two days until they reached the Dolores River. They abandoned the chase there.

Many believe Tom McCarty went to Moab and then spent some time in the LaSal Mountains, where he had relatives and friends. Since there was no money from the robbery, he probably dug up some of the cash he'd buried before the robbery. It was the McCartys' practice to take only the cash they needed before a raid; they would bury the rest and retrieve it later. Tom had plenty of time to think about the botched Delta robbery and what went wrong. He probably blamed Fred, who had participated in a couple of robberies but was young and inexperienced. Why wasn't he left with the horses while the robbery veterans, Tom and Bill, went into the bank?

Tom McCarty left the LaSals and boarded the Denver and Rio Grande train at Thompson Springs, Utah, heading to Salt Lake City. No one noticed when he bought a Union Pacific ticket north to familiar territory in Oregon.

After the commotion died down in Delta, Ray Simpson, the sharpshooter, was lauded as a hero and received many awards. The *Denver Times* presented him with a gold medal engraved with, "For his courageous acts on September 7, 1893." However, this fame had a dark side, and threatening letters were left on the hedge near his front gate so he'd see them when he left his house.

His wife and children were also threatened, so Simpson eventually sold the hardware store and moved to California. His wife was so upset by the threats that she was placed in a sanitarium, where she remained for the rest of her life. Mary Blachly, the widow of the bank cashier, supported her eight sons by giving piano lessons, and she managed to put all of them through college.

With his life a shambles, Tom took the time to evaluate just how he'd gotten to this point. When he was about ten years old, his family left Iowa to go west. His father, Alexander McCarty, was a physician, who envisioned himself as a cattleman and dreamed of having a ranch in the West. When the Civil War ended, the doctor packed up his family, left their home, and headed for the Montana Territory. The doctor also took his prize Thoroughbreds, which were to be the breeding stock for the herd he planned to build.

Dr. McCarty settled his family on fine pastureland and began raising horses, which he sold to the army posts in Montana. After four years, he moved his profitable operation from Montana to Grass Valley, Utah Territory. There was plenty of water and grass for the horses and cattle, and once again, his herds grew.

The physician and his wife, Mary, had six children: three daughters, who helped operate their ranch, and three sons, who all turned out badly. Each son was destined to spend most of his life roaming the West, usually involved in some type of illegal activity. Tom, the oldest, was born in 1850; followed by William in 1852; and George in 1862. Their parents were respected and law-abiding citizens, but the couple's sons became outlaws who stole horses, rustled cattle, and robbed banks.

As Alexander and Mary McCarty managed their successful horse business, Bill and Tom began building their own herds of cattle. When Tom was twenty-three-years old, he married "Teenie" Christina Christiansen, the daughter of Danish parents who had converted to the Mormon religion and immigrated to Utah. Her father had multiple wives and was a bishop in the church.

Bill was the first McCarty to venture into the outlaw life after he met Frank and Jessie James. They told him to go to Missouri and join the Younger brothers if he wanted some excitement. Bill did this and ended up in prison in Minnesota after stabbing and killing his robbery partner. Next, he became a bigamist when he married Anne Perry, a sixteen-year-old circus performer. Bill already had a wife in Utah whom he'd married in January 1875. Her name was Letty Maxwell Brown, and the couple wasn't married long before he left her for the life of an outlaw.

Bill McCarty. *Delta County Historical Society*.

Bill served about four years of his life sentence and then was released and pardoned when he agreed to leave Minnesota permanently. In addition to leaving the state, he left his second wife, Anne, behind and went home to Utah and Lettie. Unfortunately, Anne became seriously ill and contacted Bill, and he rushed back to Minnesota, violating his agreement. He was arrested for parole violation, but he hired a lawyer who took his case to the Minnesota Supreme Court, where he won on a technicality. Bill was free. Anne recovered, and left Bill so he could return to Lettie, who must have been very forgiving.

Bill and Tom raised cattle around the LaSal Mountains near Moab, Utah. The brothers increased the size of their herds quickly by acquiring calves that belonged to others. They drove their herds to Ouray, Colorado, and sold the cattle to the gold miners for a profit. Their cattle enterprise was growing, but Tom's real love was raising and training fast horses. He raced them often and bet heavily, which led to trouble, because his horses didn't always win. Eventually, Tom had to sell his successful ranch to pay his gambling debts.

In his autobiography, *The History of Tom McCarty*, he wrote,

> *I was born and raised by as good parents as anyone can boast of, but fortune never seemed to favor me which I suppose was my own fault. My downfall commenced by gambling. Horse racing was the first, then other gambling games, and as we all know the company one comes in contact with was the wrong kind for teaching honesty....After losing about all, I commenced to cast around for something else.*

Casting about for something else meant stealing horses, rustling cattle, robbing banks, and hiding out.

After Tom's ranch was sold, the brothers formed the Blue Mountain Gang and became horse thieves. Their parents left Utah and eventually settled in Oregon. In 1877, Tom held up the train station east of Elko, Nevada, but he foolishly didn't wear a mask or use a disguise. He was recognized, arrested, convicted of grand larceny, and sentenced to a year in the Nevada State Penitentiary.

Upon his release from prison, Tom swore he'd never be locked up again and headed for Levan, Utah, to see his wife, Teenie, and his children. After a brief visit, he left accompanied by fourteen-year-old Willard "Willy" Christiansen, Teenie's younger brother. McCarty quickly initiated Willie into the outlaw life by rustling calves for the herd of cattle they drove to Ouray and sold. On the trip back to Utah, Tom couldn't resist stealing a herd of horses, which he and Willy drove to Levan and sold. After introducing Willie to the outlaw life, Tom took him home and dropped in for a brief visit with Teenie and his children, who were living with her parents.

Willie's life changed forever when he got into a fight with another boy and hit him in the head with a board, knocking him out. Panicked, sure he'd killed the unconscious boy, Willie fled with just his horse and a bedroll. He found work as a cowboy in the remote Uinta Basin, changed his name to "Matt Warner" and used it for much of his life.

Tom McCarty spent several years in Arizona and New Mexico, stealing horses, and holding up stages. He decided he was becoming too well known there and made plans for a future elsewhere. He bought three high-quality horses in Iowa, shipped them to New Mexico, and began training them for speed and endurance.

In 1882, Matt Warner (Willie), now eighteen years old, joined Tom and his friend Josh Swett in southern Arizona. They stole a large herd of cattle, but a posse picked up their trail and began shooting at them. The cattle stampeded, and Swett was hit in the shoulder in the gunfight. Since they were riding Tom's fast horses, they managed to get ahead of the posse and turn north to avoid the usual trails and settlers. They watched for Apaches and always looked for water holes. They covered about four hundred miles, and Swett endured the rough journey but needed medical attention.

They finally reached Lee's Ferry, which would take them across the Colorado River, and planned a brief rest before they crossed. Then they spotted dust clouds and saw that the determined Arizona posse was headed their way. They loaded their horses on the ferry quickly and bribed the ferryman to get them across the Colorado in a hurry. When they got ashore on the opposite side of the river, they kidnapped the ferryman. They took him far from the river, tied him up, and shackled him to a log so they'd have a head start before he could ever bring that posse across the Colorado River.

Normally, they would have headed for their hideout in Robbers Roost, but Swett needed a doctor, so they started for Kanab, Utah. Their horses were worn out, so they stole four fresh animals from an isolated ranch and left the others behind. It took them three days to reach Kanab and get medical help for Josh Swett, who, by then, could barely stay in his saddle. They learned that the posse from the Arizona Territory was still on their trail, so Matt and Tom decided they needed to leave immediately. Swett remained in Kanab since he couldn't travel any further. The posse arrested him for stealing a horse in Utah but did not take him back to Arizona, where he would have faced charges of rustling and assault with a deadly weapon.

Matt Warner wrote in his book *The Last of The Bandit Riders* that their escape from that posse "was like a prolonged war with us using all our cowboy tricks and knowledge of the country against the skill, cunning, and guns of those officers." Tom McCarty credited their great horses with their escape and said, "Anyone who has had any experience in the kind of business we were carrying on will know that in case of emergency a good horse may save their life."

They rode west, and Tom bought a newspaper in Salt Lake City, from which he learned that Swett had improved enough to be jailed for stealing a horse. He was not extradited to Arizona, but he did spend a year in the Utah Territorial Prison. When Swett was released, he gave up the outlaw life.

Canyon Country near Robbers Roost. *Photograph by Tom Williams.*

Instead of rustling cattle, Matt Warner and Tom McCarty bought a herd in Milford, Utah, drove the cattle west, and sold them in Frisco, a wild Utah mining town. While they were delivering the herd, Marshal Bally Sackett of Milford galloped up and arrested them for stealing the cattle they'd actually paid for. He refused to listen and hauled the furious pair in a buckboard twenty-five miles back to Milford. There the rancher verified that they'd bought and paid for his cattle, but Marshal Sackett realized the pair had money from selling that herd in Frisco. He started dreaming up ways to separate them from their cash. When they didn't try to escape, it ruined his plans to shoot them. He finally had to release Matt and Tom, but they were going to have to walk back to Frisco, because their horses had been left there.

Furious about their situation and at being unfairly arrested, Tom and Matt started walking but soon realized they were being followed. They hid their money under a railroad tie, keeping only $100, and continued walking. Soon two men rode up, and demanded their cash. Matt handed over $100, and the disappointed pair wheeled their horses around and headed back to Milford. Once the thieves were out of sight, Matt and Tom went back and retrieved their roll of cash and trudged on.

Once they had their horses again, Tom and Matt left Frisco and headed for the Snake Valley and the Ketchum Ranch, an outlaw refuge. About two days after they reached the ranch, a wagon rolled up with two men who said they were prospectors. However, they had no picks, shovels, or prospecting equipment. Matt thought the two men were fakes, and a bit of eavesdropping proved him right. Tom and Matt confronted the phony prospectors and learned they were after a reward offered for their capture. The disgusted pair wasted no time sending these men on their way.

Matt and Tom left Ketchum's and headed for Ely, Nevada, but they were caught in a fierce blizzard and struggled through deep snow to reach the town. Tom developed pneumonia and was hospitalized in Ely for two months. Matt returned to Diamond Mountain, which straddled the Colorado-Utah border and thought about going straight.

When Tom McCarty recovered, he bought some "dude clothes," and craving revenge, he learned Bally Sackett was now the town marshal in Richfield, Utah. Sackett had just purchased a valuable stallion, which he was very proud of. McCarty went to Richfield, stole the stallion, and left the marshal a nasty note.

He spent 1883 prospecting along the Colorado River and in Colorado's San Juan Mountains. Then the urge to help himself to other people's cattle became too strong, so he put his plans for an honest life on hold.

Large cattle companies were operating in the Four Corners region, where their herds roamed over thousands of acres of open range. The huge Carlisle Cattle Company had over 11,000 head around Monticello, with 5,300 calves, many of which were not branded. A cowboy like Tom could quickly build up his herd with a "long loop" and a running iron. Tom saw the opportunity and set up his cattle camp near Aztec Spring, Colorado. He developed a very profitable business selling herds of rustled cattle in Colorado's San Juan Mining District.

In 1885, Bill McCarty sold his LaSal ranch and moved to Baker County, Oregon. His new ranch was located near the point where huge cattle and horse herds were gathered every spring and sold. After these herds were sold, they were driven east to the Great Plains or railroad shipping points in Nebraska, Montana, or Kansas. By 1888, Tom was bored with rustling and switched to the more challenging job of horse stealing. Every fall, he showed up near Colorado's Lone Cone Peak with horses he'd picked up in Utah and Nevada. Then in the fall, he'd steal horses in Colorado, drive them to Nevada and Oregon and sell them there.

Meantime in Colorado, Matt Warner was racing horses with a young cowboy named Butch Cassidy. While racing in Telluride, they met Jim Clark, the town marshal, who maintained order in the booming camp while he skillfully operated on both sides of the law. They ran into Tom McCarty in Cortez, Colorado and spent time at his cattle camp near Aztec Spring, making plans for their future.

Tom McCarty. *Utah State Historical Society*.

By 1889, Tom had become friends with Jim Clark. Some historians theorize that Clark was the mastermind behind Tom McCarty's March 1889 robbery of David Moffat's First National Bank in Denver. Masquerading as "Mr. Wells," McCarty made an appointment to see David Moffat, the then-president of the Denver and Rio Grande Railroad. He said he had information about a plot to rob the bank. On March 30, a cold, blustery day, Mr. Wells was ushered into Moffat's office. He wasted no time on pleasantries; he just pulled a revolver from his pocket and pointed it at Moffat's head. He warned, "Don't move, and don't say a word. If you open your mouth, I'll shoot you right now!" This got the bank president's full attention, and when McCarty ordered him to write a check for $21,000, he did it. Then McCarty produced a bottle of liquid, which he said was nitroglycerin. As he waved it around, he told Moffat that the check had to be cashed immediately. If there was any problem, he'd shoot him and blow up the bank with everyone in it. Both cashiers had gone to lunch, leaving the teller alone. Moffat took the check to the teller and told him to cash it for Mr. Wells. As instructed, the teller handed over $1,000 in gold coins, a $10,000 bill and $10,000 in smaller bills. McCarty put the currency in his breast pocket, slipped the coins into a bag hidden in his pants, bid Moffat goodbye, walked briskly out of the bank, and disappeared. The marshal was summoned, but no trace of the robber was ever found.

A few months after Tom relieved the First National Bank in Denver of $21,000, he was finalizing plans for the robbery of the San Miguel Valley Bank in Telluride. Months were spent studying the bank, its schedules, and its employees. Escape routes were developed, places were chosen to station the relay horses, and the fastest horses were trained for speed and endurance. Twenty-five-year-old Matt Warner and Butch Cassidy were amateurs at bank robbery, and Tom, who was nearing forty years of age, was their teacher. This robbery would be twenty-three-year-old Butch Cassidy's debut as an outlaw.

On June 24, 1889, Matt Warner, Tom McCarty, and Butch Cassidy rode into Telluride to make a sizable withdrawal from the bank. About 10:00 a.m., the three cowboys rode up to the bank, where Warner and Cassidy dismounted and walked inside. The third man, Tom McCarty, stayed in the saddle and held the horses by the entrance. Inside, Matt pulled his six-shooter and waved it in the cashier's face while Butch jumped over the partition and cleaned out the cash drawers. They grabbed the money from the open vault, warned the cashier not to give the alarm for at least ten minutes, and walked out the door. They jumped on their horses and galloped up Main Street, whooping and shooting their revolvers in the air.

As they dashed down the road from Telluride, they encountered Henry Adsit, who recognized Butch. The robbers raced by, puzzling Adsit until he met the posse who was chasing them. When the outlaws left the trail and took off galloping across the rough country, the posse turned back. The robbers switched horses at the relay points and kept up a steady pace, reaching Mud Springs about 10:00 p.m. They'd covered eighty miles in twelve hours, and the well-planned robbery had gone off without a hitch. They divided the take from the robbery, about $24,000, and split up.

After the robbery, Matt and Tom hid out in Brown's Park and Robbers Roost and then went to Wyoming. They spent the winter of 1889–90 in remote Star Valley, a hideout for outlaws and polygamists. Unexpectedly, Matt married fourteen-year-old Rose Morgan, and Tom, now a widower, married Sarah Lehmberg. His first wife, Teenie, Matt's sister, had died in 1881. Tom had never been much of a husband, always leaving Teenie and their children with her parents in Utah. He soon left Sarah behind, too, and went to Bill's ranch in Oregon.

Tom established himself as head of the McCarty Gang, which included his younger brother, George, and his wife, Nellie. When they decided to rob banks, their first target was the Wallowa National Bank in Enterprise, Washington, seventy miles north of Bill's ranch. On October 8, 1891, there were no customers in the bank when Matt and Bill entered. When the cashier refused to open the safe, Bill jammed his revolver against his head and snarled, "If you don't, you die right here!" The cashier quickly complied and handed over three sacks of coins. When Matt demanded currency, the cashier said there wasn't any, although he'd hidden a large amount of money under a ledger.

Since their Enterprise take was only $3,450 in coins, the brothers robbed the Summerville, Oregon bank of $4,800 a month later. Then they targeted the Rosalyn, Washington bank, which was holding the local coal company's $50,000 payroll. However, nothing went right with this robbery. Citizens spotted the action at the bank and came running as the sheriff took a couple of shots at Tom, who was holding the horses. Matt and Bill hastily collected the loot and dashed out the door, where they jumped on their horses and galloped out of town.

The getaway didn't go smoothly either. They got lost in the fog and rode in circles, missing the relay horses. Fred dropped his gun and shot himself in the leg, so he had to see a doctor. When they reached the Columbia River, they stole a boat, but it had no oars, so they used heavy planks to row across the river. The horses were towed behind, but Matt rode his and almost drowned in the Columbia. When they reached their hideout, they discovered that instead of a take of $50,000, they'd gotten only $5,000, which did not go far when split up. Their advance information had been wrong; the payroll had been delivered directly to the mine, not the bank. A posse was on their trail, and Matt's sister-in-law threatened to go to the sheriff about his part in the bank robberies. Furious, he swore he'd cut off her nose and ears if that happened. She fled to Salt Lake City and told the police chief what she knew, and this was verified by Rose, Matt's angry wife.

Tom escaped to Colorado, and by 1897, he was rustling cattle with Butch Cassidy and hiding out in Brown's Park and Robbers Roost. There was a concerted effort by the governors of Utah, Colorado, and Wyoming to put these outlaws out of business, while bounty hunters like Tom Horn kept them on the run. Tom McCarty had a $13,000 price on his head, making him the most sought-after outlaw of that time. He could not return to Utah, because he was well known there, and there was a $2,500 reward on his head for robbing David Moffat's bank in Denver.

By 1900, Tom McCarty was fifty years old and tired of running. He thought his old haunts in northeastern Oregon would be safe and returned to Wallowa County, where the statute of limitations for robberies was running out. He did some prospecting; joined the Joseph, Oregon Bachelor's Club; and even appeared in a group photograph on May 1, 1901. He was appointed county road commissioner in 1902, was director of the school board, and was elected justice of the peace in 1912. By 1917, Tom McCarty had faded out of sight and where or when he died is unknown.

His autobiography, *Tom McCarty's Own Story, Autobiography of an Outlaw* was published by Charles Kelly in 1986.

Author's Note: Doc Shores wrote in Memoirs of a Lawman *that Jim Clark asked him to contact David Moffat about exchanging one $10,000 bill for an equal amount in small denomination bills. Clark said that Doc could keep $1,000 for his trouble. Doc replied that he'd contact Moffat but that did he not want any money for himself. He was making the arrangements for the exchange when Jim Clark was assassinated. Shores told Moffat that negotiations for the $10,000 bill were over.*

12

MATT WARNER FINALLY GOES STRAIGHT

Matt Warner always said that he was pushed into the outlaw life by an incident that occurred when he was a teenager. Willard "Willie" Erastus Christianson was born in Ephriam, Utah, in 1864 to a Danish father and German mother. His parents converted to the Mormon religion, left Denmark, and immigrated to Utah. His father acquired multiple wives and became a bishop in the church.

One evening, when fourteen-year-old-year old Willie got into a fight with another boy, he grabbed a piece of wood and hit his rival in the head, knocking him unconscious. Certain he'd killed the youth, Willie raced home, snatched some clothes and a loaf of bread, and yelled goodbye to his parents. He jumped on his horse, raced out of town, and made it through Ute territory to Brown's Park in Colorado. Along the way, he decided to change his name to "Matt Warner," but the local cowboys dubbed him the "Mormon Kid."

Willie, using the name Matt, was hired as a cowboy at Jim Warren's ranch and, through diligent practice, became a tough bronc buster and a sharpshooter. His boss built his herd of cattle by gathering unbranded calves, called "slicks," whipping out his running iron and correcting that. He told his young cowhands that he wanted to help them improve their lot, and this was a quick way for them to acquire cattle and establish their own herds. Matt followed Warren's example and started his herd on Diamond Mountain, near Brown's Park.

Matt eventually learned that the boy he thought he'd killed when he was a teenager had not died. For years, he'd believed he was a murderer and was shocked when he learned that he wasn't. In his memoir, *The Last of the Bandit Riders*, he said, "When I found out I wasn't a murderer, it was too late: life had already made an outlaw out of me."

Matt's thirteen-year-old nephew, Lew McCarty, showed up one day, ready to become an outlaw. He'd stolen a gun, horse and saddle from his family and was intrigued by a scheme dreamed up by nineteen-year-old Elzy Lay. A Rock Springs, Wyoming merchant had gone broke, and the sheriff was going to seize all his merchandise and sell it to repay his creditors. The bankrupt merchant loaded all his clothing and goods into a wagon and hurried out of town. Matt and Lew, wearing masks, hid in the trees along the trail, and when the merchant went by, they jumped out, guns drawn. They took everything he had in the wagon—women's clothing, shoes, boots, jewelry, and cowboy goods—stuffed it into bags and dashed off, whooping and hollering.

Matt decided, "The only right and manly thing to do was to give them goods to the poor and lowly in the park." They gave the loot to John Jarvie, who operated a combination store/trading post in Brown's Park and told him to distribute everything to the poor people. He was to invite everyone to a masquerade party and dance and to come dressed in the "hot items." Jarvie did a good job organizing the dance, and everyone turned out. Matt described the festivities in his memoir:

> *It ain't on record either that anybody refused to take the stolen goods. Every last man, woman, child, and dog in the valley...come to the dance dressed in them cheap, misfitting clothes....It was the funniest sight I ever saw in my life....Most of the people persisted in hanging onto parts of their old cowboy and rancher outfits and mixing up clothes dreadfully.*

He continued, "The way store clothes and cowboy clothes, celluloid collars and red bandana handkerchiefs, old busted ten-gallon range hats and cheap derbies, high-heel boots and brogans, Prince Albert coats and chaps, and spurs and guns was mixed up would give you the willies." He described a wrinkled old rancher who was dressed like a minister but wore his six-shooter and belt strapped over his long, black frock coat. A cowboy sporting a gambler's bright green vest and high hat completed his outfit with leather chaps, high-heel boots, and spurs. Matt recalled, "There was a weather-beaten ranch woman, with a tanned face, and hands like a ditch digger, in a bridal veil and dress with a long train. A big cowgirl wearing a cheap gingham dress, and brogans come with a hat on that looked like a flower garden." He continued, "There was a lot of hollering and laughing and clapping and stomping, and there was so much noise and fun you couldn't hear yourself think. The party kept up that-a-way till daylight and everybody was wore out." Everyone in Brown's Park talked about that party for weeks after.

Matt Warner (born Willard Christianson), outlaw and lawman, circa 1878. *Utah State Historical Society*.

After about five years of rustling, Matt had a small ranch with his own cattle on Diamond Mountain. He built a herd of horses through rustling, trading, and breeding and developed some very fast animals. He knew cowboys who were working in Brown's Park, which had become a refuge for outlaws. Most of the small ranchers and homesteaders living there were friendly and nonjudgmental and welcomed outlaws. They could get food and supplies, swap their tired horses for fresh ones, and rest a few days because lawmen rarely ventured into Brown's Park.

Matt began racing horses in local contests, often for Charlie Crouse of Brown's Park, who owned some fine Thoroughbreds. He built a winning record and traveled around Colorado, racing, and betting against the local champions. Around 1885, when he was about twenty-one years old, he met a young cowboy named Cassidy in Telluride. Known to everyone as Butch, the youth was a fierce competitor in horse races and often won. He'd changed his name from Robert LeRoy Parker to Butch Cassidy, taking the last name of an old rustler friend. He acquired his first name while working in a Wyoming butcher shop.

Cassidy and Warner became friends and formed a partnership, racing horses in Colorado and southern Utah. One of Warner's horses named "Betty" was unbeaten, and after a big race in Cortez, he and Butch celebrated their win with Tom McCarty. This was McCarty's first meeting with Butch Cassidy and the beginning of the trio's partnership in the outlaw business. When Matt's younger sister, fifteen-year-old Christina "Teenie" Marie Christiansen, married Tom McCarty around 1873, he acquired a seasoned outlaw as a brother-in-law. The trio would soon plan a bank robbery.

During the early 1880s, Matt was increasing the size of his herd and supplementing his income by stealing horses and selling them in Wyoming.

Around 1882, Matt and cowboy Joe Brooks went to Arizona and held up a combination store and bank in St. Johns, Arizona, netting the princely sum of $897. An unexpected chase by a local posse ran the pair all the way back to Robbers Roost in Utah, where they holed up for a couple of months.

They eventually left the hideout, and Brooks headed back to Diamond Mountain while Matt went in search of his brother-in-law, Tom McCarty. He found Tom in southern Arizona, where he and cowboy Josh Swett were stealing cattle. Matt joined them, and they ran into a posse who chased them clear out of Arizona. Tom and Matt headed for California, but a series of misadventures put Tom in a Nevada hospital, while Matt returned to Diamond Mountain.

In 1888, Tom, Matt, and Butch Cassidy got together in Tom's camp near Cortez. McCarty had a profitable rustling business, but he was getting bored. The trio started planning to rob a bank in booming Telluride. On June 24, 1889, Matt, Tom McCarty, and Butch rode into Telluride and stopped at the San Miguel Valley Bank. They were ready for a good time in town, sporting ten-gallon hats, flashy shirts and bright bandanas, chaps, and cowboy boots with shiny spurs. They dismounted, and Tom waited in front with the horses, while Matt and Butch entered the bank. Matt went to the cashier's cage holding a check, as if he wanted to cash it, while Cassidy waited a few feet away. When the teller leaned forward to look at the check, Matt grabbed him, pulled his gun and jammed it against the cashier's head. The terrified man was the only employee in the bank and quickly emptied the cash drawers, handing the money to Butch. Then Matt ordered him to wait at least ten minutes before yelling for help. They walked calmly out of the bank, got on their horses, and rode up Pine Street. At the edge of town, they broke into a gallop, whooping and hollering, and shooting their guns as they headed for the mountains. They passed cattleman Henry Adsit on the trail but didn't stop to talk.

They had stationed relay horses along their getaway route, and they left $2,200 under a log by the trail for Jim Clark, Telluride's city marshal. This was his share for being conveniently out of town the day of the robbery. By the time Telluride's Sheriff Wasson got a posse organized, the bank robbers were long gone. Butch headed west into Utah, where he had friends and family, while Matt and Tom started for Brown's Park. Their haul was about $24,000, and they split it three ways. The robbery went off without a hitch, and they smugly began calling themselves the "Invincible Three."

Sheriff Wasson kept a close watch on anyone who left town, and about six days after the robbery, saloon owner Bill Madden rode out of Telluride

Lower Robbers Roost Canyon. *Photograph by Tom Williams.*

with a packhorse loaded with supplies. The sheriff followed and arrested him. By this time, Tom and Matt had already reached Brown's Park. There were rumors that a posse was headed their way, so they decided to go west to Robbers Roost.

After several weeks in this isolated hideout, they were itching to spend some of that stolen money, so they rode north to Lander, Wyoming. A posse arrived in town shortly after they got comfortable in a saloon, so they wasted no time galloping off to Star Valley. This remote corner of Wyoming on the border with Idaho was a refuge for polygamists and outlaws. The residents posted lookouts along all the roads to give a warning if anyone was coming.

The winter of 1889–90 was severe, and drifts of deep snow closed the passes out of Star Valley, keeping the pair marooned for months. Matt, who was about twenty-five years old, decided to give domestic life a try and proposed to pretty fourteen-year-old Rose Morgan. Tom McCarty loudly argued that a woman didn't fit into any outlaw's vagabond life. Then he became involved with twenty-five-year-old Sarah Lumhberg, and the two couples were married by a Mormon bishop in Montpelier, Idaho.

Matt and Tom took their wives on a honeymoon to Jackson Hole and then on to Butte City, Montana Territory. Their celebrations used the last of the Telluride cash, so the grooms sent their brides home to their parents in

Star Valley. Then they held up the Butte Saloon and gambling hall, grabbed $1,800 and dashed out of town with a posse on their heels. They headed for Bill McCarty's ranch in eastern Oregon. This was a good place to lay low and discuss the difficulties of making a living stealing horses and robbing banks. They'd been successful in Telluride, so they decided to give robbing banks another try.

Tom planned their first bank robbery carefully, targeting the Wallowa National Bank in Enterprise, Washington. Matt, Tom, and Bill, Tom's younger brother, pulled off the holdup on October 8, 1891, and their take was $3,450 in gold and silver coins. A month later Fred, Bill, and Tom robbed the small bank in Summerville, Oregon, of $4,800. In the spring of 1892, their plans to rob the casino at Hotel Warshaur in Baker City were thwarted by a rainstorm and a deputy who suddenly appeared.

Their first attempt at a train robbery on April 27, 1892, failed. They blocked the railroad tracks with boulders and timber and then waited for the Union Pacific train. When the engineer spotted the barricade and the masked men, he opened the throttle, sped up the train, and blasted through the barricade.

Then the gang received a tip that the Sumpter Valley Railroad would be carrying a large shipment of gold. Tom, Matt, and Bill barricaded the tracks with rocks and timbers near a bridge over a river. Their plan worked perfectly; the train stopped, and the express agent opened the safe. They collected gold dust, nuggets, and $3,000, which is about $60,000 today.

In September 1892, Matt, Bill, Fred, Tom, and George robbed the Rosalyn, Washington bank, which did not net them the $50,000 coal company payroll they expected. Their information was wrong; the payroll had been delivered directly to the coal mine, and their take was $5,000. The getaway did not go smoothly, and when Matt rode his horse across the Columbia River, he almost drowned. Matt was having marital troubles with his wife, Rose, and his sister-in-law threatened to report the gang's robberies to the sheriff. Matt furiously replied that if she did, he'd cut off her nose and ears. She fled to Salt Lake City and went to the police with her story.

In April 1893, Matt and George McCarty, Tom's youngest brother, were arrested for the Roslyn Bank robbery. There were warrants for Tom and Bill, who escaped to Utah. Their case wasn't helped by the interviews given by Matt's wife, Rose, and her sister, Sarah. The ladies talked freely to a reporter and told him all about the robberies that had been carried out by the McCartys and Matt Warner. The newspapers carried these interviews and accounts of every robbery.

After his arrest, Matt contacted a law firm to arrange his defense. The lawyers told him it "would take lots of money," but if he could pay their fees, they'd guarantee his freedom. After every robbery, Matt had buried much of his share of the loot, hoping to save enough to buy land or a small ranch. He made maps of the hiding places and always gave copies to Rose. Now, he drew maps for his lawyers.

On May 20, Matt and George broke a hole through the Rosalyn jail's brick wall with a crowbar and escaped. Earlier someone had slipped revolvers to them, so they were armed. A citizen recognized them and yelled for help. There was a gunfight, and one man was wounded. Both Matt and George suffered minor buckshot wounds. They were returned to jail, and Matt's trial began the following day.

Matt had hired a skillful lawyer, who discredited the prosecution witnesses, and after two days of deliberation, the jury was unable to reach a verdict. George's trial had the same outcome, but both men were still held on charges of jail break and attempted manslaughter. On September 6, 1893, that trial began, and they were dumbfounded when the judge discharged their case at the end of the first day. He said there wasn't enough evidence for the conviction of either man.

After he was released, Matt learned that most of the money he'd hidden was gone. The lawyers had found the cash, and they used $41,000 for his defense. He had $5,000 left and said it had taken him "ten years of honest-to-gawd stealin' to gather that money!" When Matt returned to his cabin, he found it had been torn apart by people looking for "robber gold." Bitter

An illustration of a bank robbery. *Vermont Historical Society*.

Posse men unload their horses in Wilcox after the June 2, 1899 train robbery. *American Heritage Center, University of Wyoming.*

about his situation, he traded his cattle and the entire ranch for a horse, saddle, and tack and headed back to Diamond Mountain.

In 1896, Matt was hired by two prospectors, Henry Coleman and Bob Swift, to guard their gold mine from thieves and claim jumpers. On the way to the mine in the Uintah Mountains, they were ambushed by three thieves: Ike and Dick Staunton and Dick Milton. Matt's horse was shot from beneath him, but he managed to kill Milton and Bill Staunton and shoot Ike in the knee, while another bullet grazed his nose. Matt summoned the sheriff, who promptly arrested him, Henry Coleman, and a man named Bill Wall for killing the two thieves. They were all jailed in Vernal, Utah, and then Wall and Matt were transferred to Ogden. This was a precaution because the sheriff had learned that Butch Cassidy and Elzy Lay were planning a jail break to free Matt. There were also threats that a Vernal lynch mob was planning to hang the pair. Matt sent a message to Butch that he needed an attorney and was desperate for money to pay one.

During the first week of August 1896, Butch, "Bub" Meeks, and Elzy Lay studied the Montpelier, Idaho bank, its schedule, and the employees' routine. Then on August 13, the three outlaws robbed the bank and stole between $7,000 and $9,000, which is about $225,000 today. After grabbing the cash, they galloped out of town and easily outran a pursuing posse. Cassidy hired a lawyer in Rock Springs, Wyoming, who arranged for a Utah

Matt Warner in prison, 1897. *Utah State Historical Society.*

lawyer to handle Matt's case. Despite the efforts of his friends, Matt was charged with murder but tried and convicted of manslaughter. He was sentenced to five years in the Utah Territorial Prison.

While Matt was in prison, his pregnant wife, Rose, developed bone cancer. When her baby boy was born, she was too ill to care for him and moved in with her parents in Salt Lake City. Rose died in the fall of 1896, and Matt was allowed to attend her funeral. He recalled in his memoir, "I guess a man never went through more agony and lived than I did when they took me handcuffed between two guards to see my dead wife lying there in the coffin and that weak, puny, shriveled, half-dead baby in the arms of its accusing grandmother. That was my past, all my responsibility rising up all together and handing me a knockout right on the chin."

Matt realized that he was paying the price now for living the way he had for years. He decided that he wanted to get out of the outlaw life for good. He later wrote in his memoir, "Your whole outlaw past is just one big trap, just one big spider's web, that has purty [*sic*] near a death grip on you, and you have one hell of a time breaking out." He served three years and four months in prison and promised to go straight. He was pardoned by the governor of Utah and released from prison.

Matt eventually remarried and settled in Carbon County, Utah. He ran for the office of justice of the peace using his birth name, Willard Erastus Christiansen, and he lost because nobody knew him by that name. He had his name legally changed to Matt Warner, ran again, and was elected justice of the peace of Price, Utah. Matt later served as a deputy sheriff and a detective, and after retirement, he worked as a night guard. His memoir, *The Last of the Bandit Riders*, was serialized and appeared in *Cosmopolitan* a few months before he died on December 21, 1938. He was seventy-four years old. In November 2000, *The Last of the Bandit Riders*: *Revisited*, by Joyce Warner and Steve Lacy was published, with photographs and maps added to the original text.

BIBLIOGRAPHY

Brockett, D.A. *Wicked Western Slope*. Charleston, SC: The History Press, 2012.

Carlson, Chip. *Tom Horn: Blood on the Moon*. Glendo, WY: High Plains Press, 2001.

Colton, Ray C. *The Civil War in the Western Territories*. Norman: The University of Oklahoma Press, 1959.

Cook, D.J. (general). *Hands Up*. Norman: University of Oklahoma Press, 1958.

Drago, Harry. *The Legend Makers*. New York: Dodd, Mead & Co., 1975.

Dyer, John Lewis. *The Snowshoe Itinerant.* Cincinnati, OH: Cranston and Stowe, 1890.

Eberle, Jeff. *The Reynolds Gang Unmasked: The Legend, The Truth, The Treasure.* Central City, CO: Life, Death, Iron Publishing, 2023.

Gallagher, Jolie. *A Wild West History of Frontier Colorado*. Charleston, SC: The History Press, 2011.

Gay, Heath. *Forgotten Colorado Southern Region*. Charleston, SC: Arcadia Publishing, 2021.

Jessen, Ken. *Colorado Gunsmoke*. Loveland, CO: JV Publications, 1986.

Jocknick, Sidney. *Early Days on the Western Slope of Colorado*. Lake City, CO: Western Reflections, 1998.

Jones, Adam. *The Vendetta of Felipe Espinosa*. Farmington Hills, MI: Gale, 2014.

Kelly, Charles. *The Outlaw Trail.* Lincoln: University of Nebraska Press, 1939.

Kouris, Diana. *Nighthawk Rising*. Glendo, WY: High Plains Press, 2019.

———. *The Romantic and Notorious History of Brown's Park*. Greybull, WY: Wolverine Gallery, 1988.

Leonard, Stephen J. *Lynching in Colorado 1859–1919*. Boulder: University Press of Colorado, 2002.

Marriott, Barbara. *Outlaws of New Mexico*. Kearney, NE: Morris Publishing, 2017.

McClure, Grace. *The Bassett Women*. Athens, OH: Swallow Press, 1985.

McConnell, Virginia. *Bayou Salado*. Boulder: University Press of Colorado, 1966.

Monaghan, Jay. *The Legend of Tom Horn: The Last of the Bad Men*. New York: Bobs-Merrill Company, 1946.

———. *Tom Horn: Last of the Bad Men*. Lincoln: University of Nebraska Press, 1946.

O'Neal, Bill. *Encyclopedia of Western Gunfighters*. Norman: University of Oklahoma Publishing, 1979.

Parkhill, Forbes. *The Law Goes West*. Thousand Oaks, CA: Sage, 1956.

Perkins, James. *Tom Tobin: Frontiersman*. Pueblo, CO: Herodotus Press, 1999.

Price, Charles. *Season of Terror*. Boulder: University Press of Colorado, 2013.

Rockwell, Wilson. *Doc Shores, Memoirs of a Lawman*. Lake City, CO: Western Reflections Publishing, 2012.

———. *Uncompahgre Country*. Lake City, CO: Western Reflections Publishing, 1965.

Ruland-Thorne, Kate. *Historic Tales of Colorado's Grand Valley*. Charleston, SC: The History Press, 2016.

Sammons, Judy. *Keepin' the Peace*. Lake City, CO: Western Reflections Publishing, 2010.

Silbernagel, Robert. *Historic Adventures on the Colorado Plateau*. Charleston, SC: The History Press, 2018.

Skovlin, Jon, and Donna Skovlin. *In Pursuit of the McCartys*. Bend, OR: Maverick Publications, 2001.

Smith, Duane. *The Birth of Colorado: A Civil War Perspective*. Norman: University of Oklahoma Press, 1989.

———. *Crested Butte from Coal Camp to Ski Town*. Lake City, CO: Western Reflections Publishing, 2008.

Turner, Carol. *The Notorious San Juans*. Charleston, SC: The History Press, 2011.

Warner, Matt, and Murray E. King. *The Last of the Bandit Riders*. New York: Bonanza Books, 1940.

Wetzel, James. *Banks, Bullets, and Bodies*. Delta, CO: Self-published, 2020.

Wommack, Linda. *Ann Bassett: Colorado's Cattle Queen*. Caldwell, ID: Caxton Press, 2018.

INDEX

D

E

F

G

H

I

J

K

L

M

N

T

U

W

ABOUT THE AUTHOR

Nancy has spent her life in the West and has always been fascinated by its history. She has written numerous articles and six books about the American frontier, its visionaries and its people, their courage, endurance and dreams. She lives in Colorado, where history is nearby in the state's historic buildings and old mining camps, reminders of a dynamic time.

Visit us at
www.historypress.com